WORLD ATLAS

CONTENTS

Collins World Atlas, first published 1986 by William Collins Sons & Co. Ltd.,
P.O. Box, Glasgow G4 0NB
Reprinted 1987, 1988, 1989
New Edition 1990

Collins World Atlas
© William Collins Sons & Co. Ltd. 1986, 1990

Maps © William Collins Sons & Co. Ltd. 1983, 1984, 1985, 1986, 1990
and © Collins-Longman Atlases 1969-1983, 1984, 1985, 1986 and 1990

Prepared and designed by Collins Cartographic under the direction of Andrew M Currie, M.A., Managing Editor.

Printed and bound in Scotland by William Collins Sons & Co. Ltd.

ISBN 0 00 447703 0

COLLINS

LONDON · GLASGOW · SYDNEY · AUCKLAND · NEW YORK · TORONTO · JOHANNESBURG

Earth's Dimensions

Superficial area	510 066 000 km²
Land surface	148 326 000 km²
Water surface	361 740 000 km²
Equatorial circumference	40 075 km
Meridional circumference	40 007 km
Volume	$1\,083\,230 \times 10^6$ km³
Mass	5.976×10^{21} tonnes

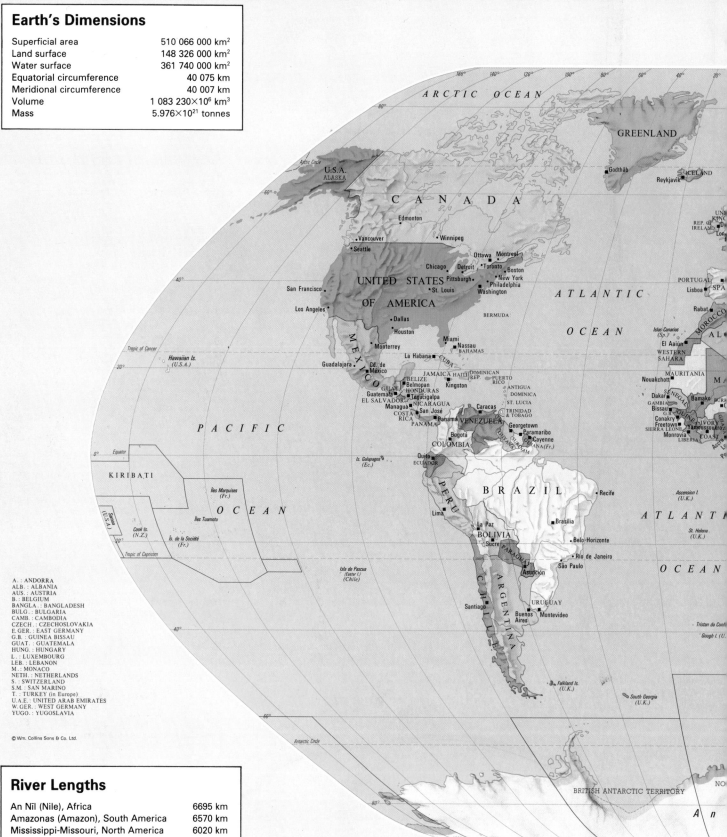

A. : ANDORRA
ALB. : ALBANIA
AUS. : AUSTRIA
B. : BELGIUM
BANGLA. : BANGLADESH
BULG. : BULGARIA
CAMB. : CAMBODIA
CZECH. : CZECHOSLOVAKIA
E. GER. : EAST GERMANY
G.B. : GUINEA BISSAU
GUAT. : GUATEMALA
HUNG. : HUNGARY
L. : LUXEMBOURG
LEB. : LEBANON
M. : MONACO
NETH. : NETHERLANDS
S. : SWITZERLAND
S.M. : SAN MARINO
T. : TURKEY (in Europe)
U.A.E. : UNITED ARAB EMIRATES
W. GER. : WEST GERMANY
YUGO. : YUGOSLAVIA

© Wm. Collins Sons & Co. Ltd.

River Lengths

An Nīl (Nile), Africa	6695 km
Amazonas (Amazon), South America	6570 km
Mississippi-Missouri, North America	6020 km
Chang Jiang (Yangtze), Asia	5471 km
Ob-Irtysh, Asia	5410 km
Huang He (Hwang Ho), Asia	4840 km
Zaïre, Africa	4630 km
Amur, Asia	4416 km
Lena, Asia	4269 km
Mackenzie, North America	4240 km
Niger, Africa	4183 km
Mekong, Asia	4180 km
Yenisey, Asia	4090 km
Murray-Darling, Oceania	3717 km
Volga, Europe	3688 km

Lake and Inland Sea Areas

Some areas are subject to seasonal variations

Caspian Sea, U.S.S.R./Iran	371 795 km²	Lake Tanganyika, East Africa	32 893 km²
Lake Superior, U.S.A./Canada	82 413 km²	Great Bear Lake, Canada	31 792 km²
Lake Victoria, East Africa	69 485 km²	Ozero Baykal (Lake Baikal), U.S.S.R.	30 510 km²
Aralskoye More (Aral Sea), U.S.S.R.	66 457 km²	Great Slave Lake, Canada	28 930 km²
Lake Huron, U.S.A./Canada	59 596 km²	Lake Malaŵi, Malaŵi/Mozambique	28 490 km²
Lake Michigan, U.S.A.	58 016 km²	Lake Erie, U.S.A./Canada	25 667 km²

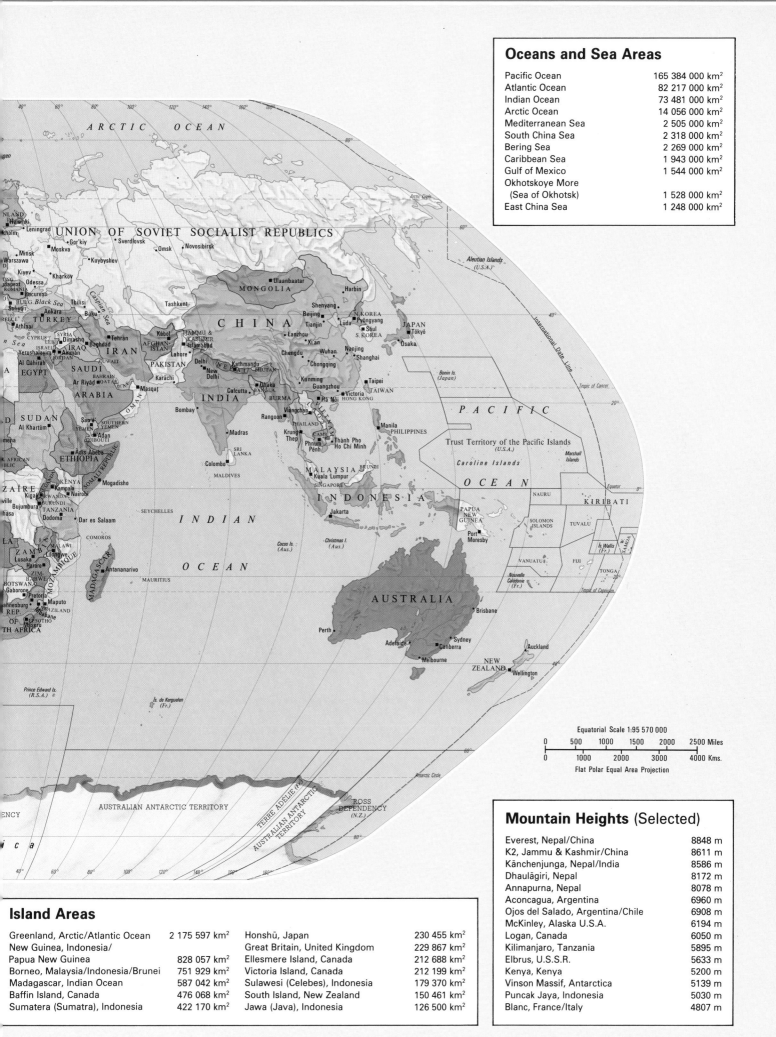

Oceans and Sea Areas

Pacific Ocean	165 384 000 km²
Atlantic Ocean	82 217 000 km²
Indian Ocean	73 481 000 km²
Arctic Ocean	14 056 000 km²
Mediterranean Sea	2 505 000 km²
South China Sea	2 318 000 km²
Bering Sea	2 269 000 km²
Caribbean Sea	1 943 000 km²
Gulf of Mexico	1 544 000 km²
Okhotskoye More (Sea of Okhotsk)	1 528 000 km²
East China Sea	1 248 000 km²

Equatorial Scale 1:95 570 000

```
0    500   1000  1500  2000  2500 Miles
0   1000  2000  3000  4000 Kms.
```
Flat Polar Equal Area Projection

Mountain Heights (Selected)

Everest, Nepal/China	8848 m
K2, Jammu & Kashmir/China	8611 m
Kānchenjunga, Nepal/India	8586 m
Dhaulāgiri, Nepal	8172 m
Annapurna, Nepal	8078 m
Aconcagua, Argentina	6960 m
Ojos del Salado, Argentina/Chile	6908 m
McKinley, Alaska U.S.A.	6194 m
Logan, Canada	6050 m
Kilimanjaro, Tanzania	5895 m
Elbrus, U.S.S.R.	5633 m
Kenya, Kenya	5200 m
Vinson Massif, Antarctica	5139 m
Puncak Jaya, Indonesia	5030 m
Blanc, France/Italy	4807 m

Island Areas

Greenland, Arctic/Atlantic Ocean	2 175 597 km²	Honshū, Japan	230 455 km²
New Guinea, Indonesia/Papua New Guinea	828 057 km²	Great Britain, United Kingdom	229 867 km²
		Ellesmere Island, Canada	212 688 km²
Borneo, Malaysia/Indonesia/Brunei	751 929 km²	Victoria Island, Canada	212 199 km²
Madagascar, Indian Ocean	587 042 km²	Sulawesi (Celebes), Indonesia	179 370 km²
Baffin Island, Canada	476 068 km²	South Island, New Zealand	150 461 km²
Sumatera (Sumatra), Indonesia	422 170 km²	Jawa (Java), Indonesia	126 500 km²

ASIA

COUNTRY	POPULATION	AREA sq. km.	CAPITAL
AFGHANISTAN	16 786 000	647 497	Kābol (Kabul)
BAHRAIN	371 000	622	Al Manāmah
BANGLADESH	92 619 000	143 998	Dhaka
BHUTAN	1 355 000	47 000	Thimbu
BRUNEI	193 000	5 765	Bandar Seri Begawan
BURMA	33 640 000	676 552	Rangoon
CAMBODIA	6 981 000	181 035	Phnum Pénh (Phnom Penh)
CHINA	1 031 883 000	9 596 961	Beijing (Peking)
CYPRUS	645 000	9 251	Levkosía (Nicosia)
HONG KONG	5 233 000	1 045	
INDIA	711 664 000	3 287 590	New Delhi
INDONESIA	151 720 000	1 904 345	Jakarta
IRAN	40 240 000	1 648 000	Tehrān
IRAQ	13 997 000	434 924	Baghdād
ISRAEL	4 022 000	20 770	Yerushalayim (Jerusalem)
JAPAN	118 449 000	372 313	Tôkyô
JORDAN	2 779 000	97 740	'Ammān
KUWAIT	1 562 000	17 818	Al Kuwayt (Kuwait)
LAOS	3 902 000	236 800	Viangchan (Vientiane)
LEBANON	2 739 000	10 400	Bayrūt (Beirut)
MALAYSIA	14 765 000	329 749	Kuala Lumpur
MALDIVES	150 000	298	Malé
MONGOLIA	1 764 000	1 565 000	Ulaanbaatar (Ulan Bator)
NEPAL	15 020 000	140 797	Kathmandu
NORTH KOREA	18 747 000	120 538	Pyŏngyang
OMAN	948 000	212 457	Masqaṭ (Muscat)
PAKISTAN	87 125 000	803 943	Islāmābād
PHILIPPINES	50 740 000	300 000	Manila
QATAR	258 000	11 000	Ad Dawḥah (Doha)
SAUDI ARABIA	9 684 000	2 149 690	Ar Riyāḍ (Riyadh)
SINGAPORE	2 472 000	620	Singapore
SOUTH KOREA	39 331 000	98 484	Sôul (Seoul)
SOUTHERN YEMEN	2 093 000	332 968	'Adan (Aden)
SRI LANKA	15 189 000	65 610	Colombo
SYRIA	9 660 000	185 180	Dimashq (Damascus)
TAIWAN	18 458 000	35 961	Taipei
THAILAND	48 450 000	514 000	Krung Thep (Bangkok)
TURKEY	46 312 000	780 576	Ankara
UNITED ARAB EMIRATES	1 043 000	83 600	
VIETNAM	56 205 000	333 000	Hà Nôi (Hanoi)
YEMEN	6 077 000	195 000	Şan 'ā'

AFRICA

COUNTRY	POPULATION	AREA sq. km.	CAPITAL
ALGERIA	20 293 000	2 381 741	Alger (Algiers)
ANGOLA	7 452 000	1 246 700	Luanda
BENIN	3 618 000	112 622	Porto-Novo
BOTSWANA	937 000	600 372	Gaborone
BURKINA	6 360 000	274 200	Ouagadougou
BURUNDI	4 460 000	27 834	Bujumbura
CAMEROON	8 865 000	475 442	Yaoundé
CAPE VERDE	329 000	4 033	Praia
CENTRAL AFRICAN REPUBLIC	2 456 000	622 984	Bangui
CHAD	4 643 000	1 284 000	N'Djamena
COMOROS	370 000	2 171	Moroni
CONGO	1 621 000	342 000	Brazzaville
DJIBOUTI	332 000	22 000	Djibouti
EGYPT	44 673 000	1 001 449	Al Qāhirah (Cairo)
EQUATORIAL GUINEA	381 000	28 051	Malabo
ETHIOPIA	32 775 000	1 221 900	Ādīs Ābeba (Addis Ababa)
GABON	563 000	267 667	Libreville
GAMBIA	635 000	11 295	Banjul
GHANA	12 244 000	238 537	Accra
GUINEA	5 285 000	245 857	Conakry
GUINEA BISSAU	810 000	36 125	Bissau
IVORY COAST	8 568 000	322 462	Yamoussoukro
KENYA	17 864 000	582 646	Nairobi
LESOTHO	1 409 000	30 355	Maseru
LIBERIA	2 113 000	111 369	Monrovia
LIBYA	3 224 000	1 759 540	Ṭarābulus (Tripoli)
MADAGASCAR	9 233 000	587 041	Antananarivo
MALAŴI	6 267 000	118 484	Lilongwe
MALI	7 342 000	1 240 000	Bamako
MAURITANIA	1 730 000	1 030 700	Nouakchott
MAURITIUS	983 000	2 045	Port Louis
MOROCCO	21 667 000	446 550	Rabat
MOZAMBIQUE	12 615 000	783 000	Maputo
NAMIBIA	852 000	824 292	Windhoek
NIGER	5 686 000	1 267 000	Niamey
NIGERIA	82 392 000	923 768	Abuja
RWANDA	5 276 000	26 338	Kigali
SÃO TOMÉ AND PRÍNCIPE	86 000	964	São Tomé
SENEGAL	5 968 000	196 192	Dakar
SEYCHELLES	64 000	280	Victoria
SIERRA LEONE	3 672 000	71 740	Freetown
SOMALI REPUBLIC	5 116 000	637 657	Mogadisho
SOUTH AFRICA, REPUBLIC OF	31 008 000	1 221 037	Cape Town (Kaapstad)/ Pretoria
SUDAN	19 451 000	2 505 813	Al Kharṭūm (Khartoum)
SWAZILAND	585 000	17 363	Mbabane
TANZANIA	17 982 000	945 087	Dodoma
TOGO	2 747 000	56 000	Lomé
TUNISIA	6 672 000	163 610	Tunis
UGANDA	13 225 000	236 036	Kampala
WESTERN SAHARA	165 000	266 000	El Aaiún
ZAÏRE	26 377 000	2 345 409	Kinshasa
ZAMBIA	5 680 000	752 614	Lusaka
ZIMBABWE	7 540 000	390 580	Harare

CITY	COUNTRY	POPULATION
NEW YORK	United States	16 479 000
CIUDAD DE MÉXICO (MEXICO CITY)	Mexico	13 994 000
TÔKYÔ	Japan	11 695 000
SHANGHAI	China	10 820 000
LOS ANGELES	United States	10 607 000
PARIS	France	9 863 000
BUENOS AIRES	Argentina	8 436 000

CITY	COUNTRY	POPULATION
MOSKVA (MOSCOW)	U.S.S.R.	8 011 000
CHICAGO	United States	7 664 000
BEIJING (PEKING)	China	7 570 000
SÃO PAULO	Brazil	7 199 000
CALCUTTA	India	7 031 000
SÔUL (SEOUL)	South Korea	6 879 000
LONDON	United Kingdom	6 696 000
BOMBAY	India	5 971 000

NORTH AMERICA

COUNTRY	POPULATION	AREA sq. km.	CAPITAL
ANTIGUA AND BARBUDA	77 000	442	St John's
BAHAMAS	218 000	13 935	Nassau
BARBADOS	249 000	431	Bridgetown
BELIZE	145 000	22 965	Belmopan
BERMUDA	55 000	53	Hamilton
CANADA	24 625 000	9 976 139	Ottawa
COSTA RICA	2 324 000	50 700	San José
CUBA	9 782 000	114 524	La Habana (Havana)
DOMINICA	81 000	751	Roseau
DOMINICAN REPUBLIC	5 744 000	48 734	Santo Domingo
EL SALVADOR	4 999 000	21 041	San Salvador
GREENLAND	52 000	2 175 600	Godthåb/Nuuk
GRENADA	113 000	344	St George's
GUATEMALA	7 699 000	108 889	Guatemala
HAITI	5 201 000	27 750	Port-au-Prince
HONDURAS	3 955 000	112 088	Tegucigalpa
JAMAICA	2 253 000	10 991	Kingston
MEXICO	73 011 000	1 972 547	Ciudad de México (Mexico City)
NICARAGUA	2 918 000	130 000	Managua
PANAMA	2 043 000	75 650	Panamá
PUERTO RICO	3 242 000	8 897	San Juan
ST KITTS-NEVIS	44 000	266	Basseterre
ST LUCIA	122 000	616	Castries
ST VINCENT AND THE GRENADINES	124 000	389	Kingstown
UNITED STATES OF AMERICA	232 057 000	9 363 123	Washington

SOUTH AMERICA

COUNTRY	POPULATION	AREA sq. km.	CAPITAL
ARGENTINA	28 432 000	2 766 889	Buenos Aires
BOLIVIA	5 916 000	1 098 581	La Paz/Sucre
BRAZIL	126 806 000	8 511 965	Brasília
CHILE	11 617 000	756 945	Santiago
COLOMBIA	28 776 000	1 138 914	Bogotá
ECUADOR	8 945 000	283 561	Quito
FALKLAND ISLANDS	2 000	12 173	Stanley
GUIANA	73 000	91 000	Cayenne
GUYANA	793 000	214 969	Georgetown
PARAGUAY	3 026 000	406 752	Asunción
PERU	18 790 000	1 285 216	Lima
SURINAM	352 000	163 265	Paramaribo
TRINIDAD AND TOBAGO	1 060 000	5 128	Port of Spain
URUGUAY	2 947 000	177 508	Montevideo
VENEZUELA	14 714 000	912 050	Caracas

EUROPE

COUNTRY	POPULATION	AREA sq. km.	CAPITAL
ALBANIA	2 858 000	28 748	Tiranë
ANDORRA	40 000	453	Andorra
AUSTRIA	7 571 000	83 849	Wien (Vienna)
BELGIUM	9 845 000	30 513	Bruxelles/ Brussel (Brussels)
BULGARIA	9 107 000	110 912	Sofiya (Sofia)
CZECHOSLOVAKIA	15 400 000	127 869	Praha (Prague)
DENMARK	5 119 000	43 069	Köbenhavn (Copenhagen)
EAST GERMANY	16 864 000	108 178	East Berlin
FINLAND	4 835 000	337 009	Helsinki
FRANCE	54 221 000	547 026	Paris
GREECE	9 793 000	131 944	Athinai (Athens)
HUNGARY	10 696 000	93 030	Budapest
ICELAND	236 000	103 000	Reykjavik
IRELAND, REPUBLIC OF	3 483 000	70 023	Dublin
ITALY	56 355 000	301 225	Roma (Rome)
LIECHTENSTEIN	26 000	157	Vaduz
LUXEMBOURG	366 000	2 586	Luxembourg
MALTA	360 000	316	Valletta
MONACO	27 000	1.5	Monaco
NETHERLANDS	14 342 000	40 844	Amsterdam
NORWAY	4 123 000	324 219	Oslo
POLAND	36 748 000	312 677	Warszawa (Warsaw)
PORTUGAL	10 056 000	92 082	Lisboa (Lisbon)
ROMANIA	22 638 000	237 500	Bucureşti (Bucharest)
SAN MARINO	21 000	61	San Marino
SPAIN	37 935 000	504 782	Madrid
SWEDEN	8 327 000	449 964	Stockholm
SWITZERLAND	6 384 000	41 288	Bern (Berne)
U.S.S.R.	269 994 000	22 402 200	Moskva (Moscow)
UNITED KINGDOM	56 459 000	244 046	London
WEST GERMANY	61 546 000	248 577	Bonn
YUGOSLAVIA	22 795 000	255 804	Beograd (Belgrade)

OCEANIA

COUNTRY	POPULATION	AREA sq. km.	CAPITAL
AUSTRALIA	15 226 000	7 686 848	Canberra
FIJI	658 000	18 272	Suva
KIRIBATI	60 000	886	Tarawa
NAURU	8 000	21	Nauru
NEW CALEDONIA	146 000	19 058	Nouméa
NEW ZEALAND	3 230 000	268 676	Wellington
PAPUA NEW GUINEA	3 094 000	461 691	Port Moresby
SOLOMON ISLANDS	246 000	28 446	Honiara
TONGA	101 000	699	Nuku'alofa
TUVALU	8 000	24	Funafuti
VANUATU	126 000	14 763	Vila
WESTERN SAMOA	159 000	2 842	Apia

Wm. Collins Sons & Co. Ltd.

Map coverage extends to every part of the world in a balanced scheme that avoids any individual country or regional bias. Map areas are chosen to reflect the social, economic, cultural or historical importance of a particular region. Each double spread or single page map has been planned deliberately to cover an entire physical or political unit. Generous map overlaps are included to maintain continuity. Each of the continents is treated systematically in a subsection of its own. As an aid to the reader in locating the required area, a postage stamp key map is incorporated into the title margin of each map page.

Map projections have been chosen to reflect the different requirements of particular areas. No map can be absolutely true on account of the impossibility of representing a spheroid accurately on a flat surface without some distortion in either area, distance, direction or shape. In a general world atlas it is the equal area property that is most important to retain for comparative map studies and feature size evaluation and this principle has been followed wherever possible in this map section.

Map scales, as expressions of the relationship which the distance between any two points of the map bears to the corresponding distance on the ground, are in the context of this atlas grouped into three distinct categories.

Large scales, of between 1 : 1 000 000 (1 centimetre to 10 kilometres or 1 inch to 16 miles) and 1 : 2 500 000 (1 centimetre to 25 kilometres or 1 inch to 40 miles), are used to cover particularly dense populated areas of Western Europe and Japan.

Medium scales, of between 1 : 2 500 000 and 1 : 7 500 000 are used for maps of important parts of Europe, North America, Australasia, etc.

Small scales, of less than 1 : 7 500 000 (e.g. 1 : 10 000 000, 1 : 15 000 000, 1 : 25 000 000 etc.), are selected for maps of the complete world, oceans and many of the larger countries.

The actual scale at which a particular area is mapped

therefore reflects its shape, size and density of detail, and as a basic principle the more detail required to be shown of an area, the greater its scale. However, throughout this atlas, map scales have been limited in number, as far as possible, in order to facilitate comparison between maps.

Map measurements give preference to the metric system which is now used in nearly every country throughout the world. All spot heights and ocean depths are shown in metres and the relief and submarine layer delineation is based on metric contour levels. However, all linear scalebar and height reference column figures are given in metric and imperial equivalents to facilitate conversion of measurements for the non-metric reader.

Map symbols used are fully explained in the legend below. Careful study and frequent reference to this legend will aid in the reader's ability to extract maximum information.

Topography is shown by the combined means of precise spot heights, contouring, layer tinting and three-dimensional hill shading.

Hydrographic features such as coastlines, rivers, lakes, swamps and canals are clearly differentiated.

Communications are particularly well represented with the contemporary importance of airports and road networks duly emphasized.

International boundaries and national capitals are fully documented and internal administrative divisions are shown with the maximum detail that the scale will allow. Boundary delineation reflects the 'de facto' rather than the 'de jure' political interpretation and where relevant an undefined or disputed boundary is distinguished. However there is no intended implication that the publishers necessarily endorse or accept the status of any political entity recorded on the maps.

Settlements are shown by a series of graded town stamps, each representing a population size category, based on the latest census figures.

Other features, such as notable ancient monuments, oases, national parks, oil and gas fields, are selectively included on particular maps that merit their identification.

Lettering styles used in the maps have been chosen with great care to ensure maximum legibility and clear distinction of named feature categories. The size and weight of the various typefaces reflect the relative importance of the features. Town names are graded to correspond with the appropriate town stamp.

Map place names have been selected in accordance with maintaining legibility at a given scale and at the same time striking an appropriate balance between natural and man-made features worthy of note. Name forms have been standardized according to the widely accepted principle, now well established in international reference atlases, of including place names and geographical terms in the local language of the country in question. In the case of non-Roman scripts (e.g. Arabic), transliteration and transcription have either been based on the rules recommended by the Permanent Committee on Geographical Names and the United States Board on Geographic Names, or as in the case of the adopted Pinyin transcription of Chinese names, a system officially proposed by the country concerned. The diacritical signs used in each language or transliteration have been retained on all the maps and throughout the index. However the English language reader's requirements have also been recognised in that the names of all countries, oceans, major seas and land features as well as familiar alternative name versions of important towns are presented in English.

Map sources used in the compilation of this atlas were many and varied, but always of the latest available information. At each stage of their preparation the maps were submitted to a thorough process of research and continual revision to ensure that on publication all data would be as accurate as practicable. A well-documented data bank was created to ensure consistency and validity of all information represented on the maps.

Relief

		Feet	Relief	Metres
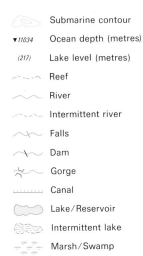	Land contour	16404		5000
▲ 8848	Spot height (metres)	9843		3000
⋈	Pass	6562		2000
	Permanent ice cap	3281		1000
		1640		500
		656		200
		0 Land Dep.	Sea Level	
		656		200
		13123		4000
		22966		7000

Hydrography

- Submarine contour
- ▼11034 Ocean depth (metres)
- (217) Lake level (metres)
- Reef
- River
- Intermittent river
- Falls
- Dam
- Gorge
- Canal
- Lake/Reservoir
- Intermittent lake
- Marsh/Swamp

© Wm. Collins Sons & Co. Ltd.

SYMBOLS

Administration

- —— International boundary
- --- Undefined/Disputed international boundary
- —·—·— Internal division : First order
- —··—··— Internal division : Second order
- National capitals

Settlement

Each settlement is given a town stamp according to its population size and scale category.

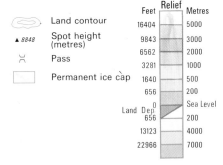

	1:1M-1:2½M	2½M-1:7½M	1:7½M or smaller
	over 1 000 000	over 1 000 000	over 1 000 000
◉	500 000-1 000 000	500 000-1 000 000	500 000-1 000 000
◎	100 000-500 000	100 000-500 000	100 000-500 000
⊙	25 000-100 000	25 000-100 000	under 100 000
○	10 000-25 000	under 25 000	—
•	under 10 000	—	—
	Major urban area (1:1M-1:2½M only)		

The size of type used for each settlement is graded to correspond with the appropriate town stamp.

Communications

- Main railway (Tunnel)
- ✈ Main airport
- - - - Track

Road representation varies with the scale category.

- Principal road
- Other main road } 1:1M-1:2½M

- Principal road
- Other main road } 1:2½M-1:7½M

- Principal road 1:7½M or smaller

Other features

- ∴ Ancient monument
- ⌣ Oasis
- National Park
- ▲ Oil field
- △ Gas field
- Oil/Gas pipeline

Lettering

Various styles of lettering are used - each one representing a different type of feature.

ALPS	Physical feature	KENYA	Country name
Red Sea	Hydrographic feature	IOWA	Internal division
Paris	Settlement name	*(Fr.)*	Territorial administration

BRITISH ISLES

ENGLAND AND WALES

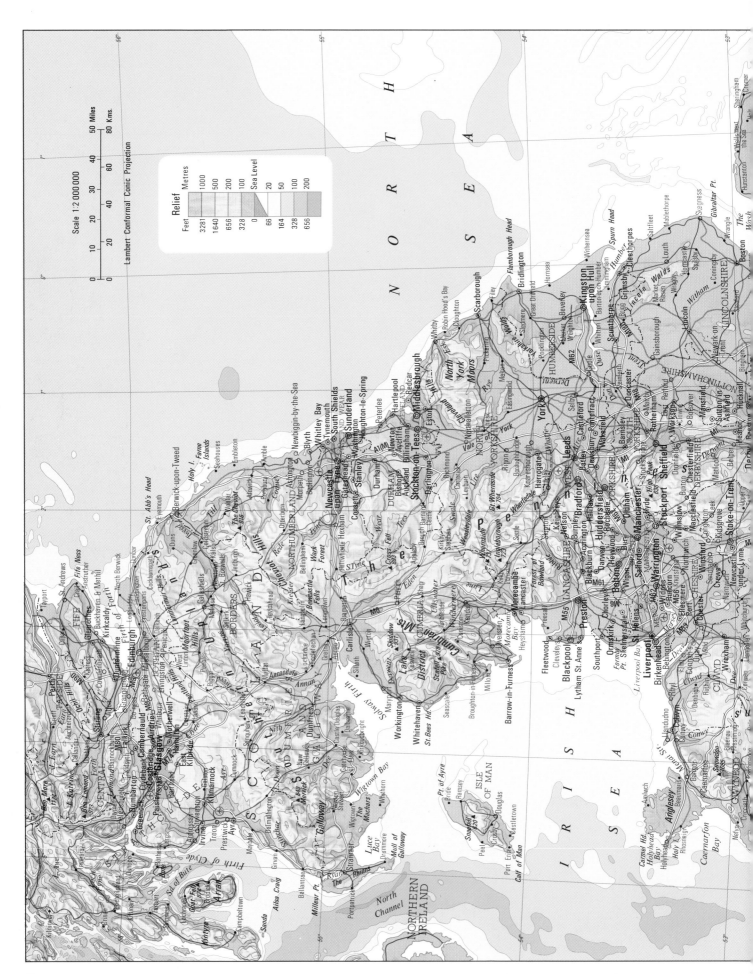

Scale 1:2 000 000

Lambert Conformal Conic Projection

50 Miles
80 Kms.

Relief
Metres
1000 500 200 100 0 Sea Level 20 50 100 200
Feet
3281 1640 656 328 0 66 164 328 656

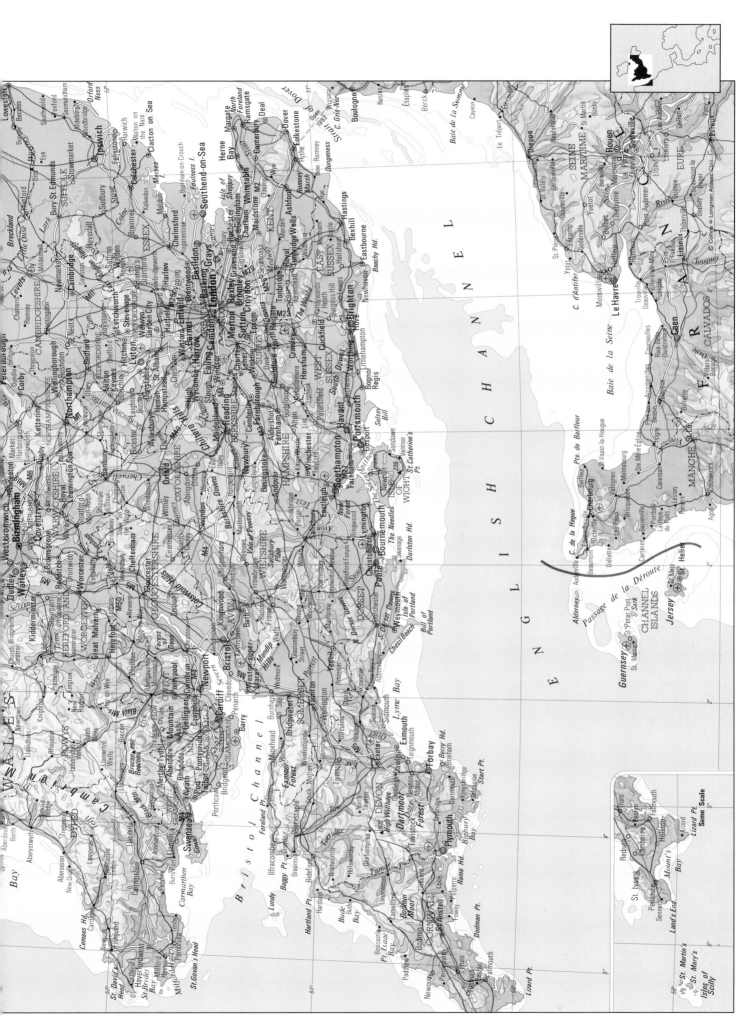

Relief

Feet	Metres
3281	1000
1640	500
656	200
328	100
0	Sea Level
66	20
164	50
328	100
656	200

Scale 1 : 2 000 000

0   10   20   30   40 Miles

0   20   40   60 Kms.

Lambert Conformal Conic Projection

© Collins ◇ Longman Atlases Cbiii

SCOTLAND

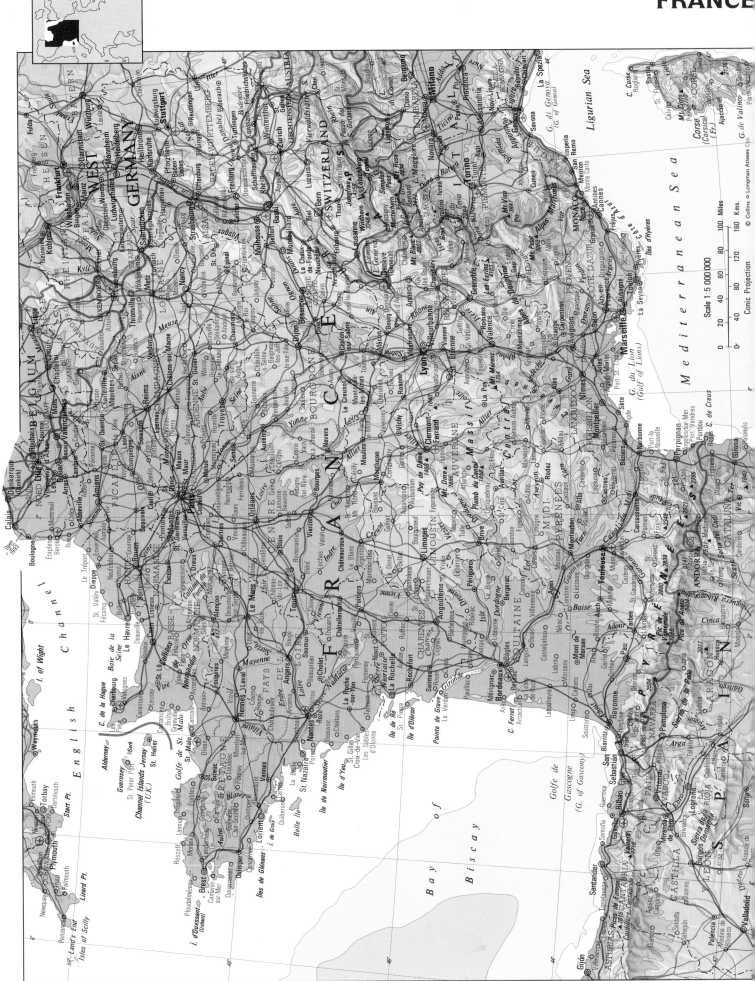

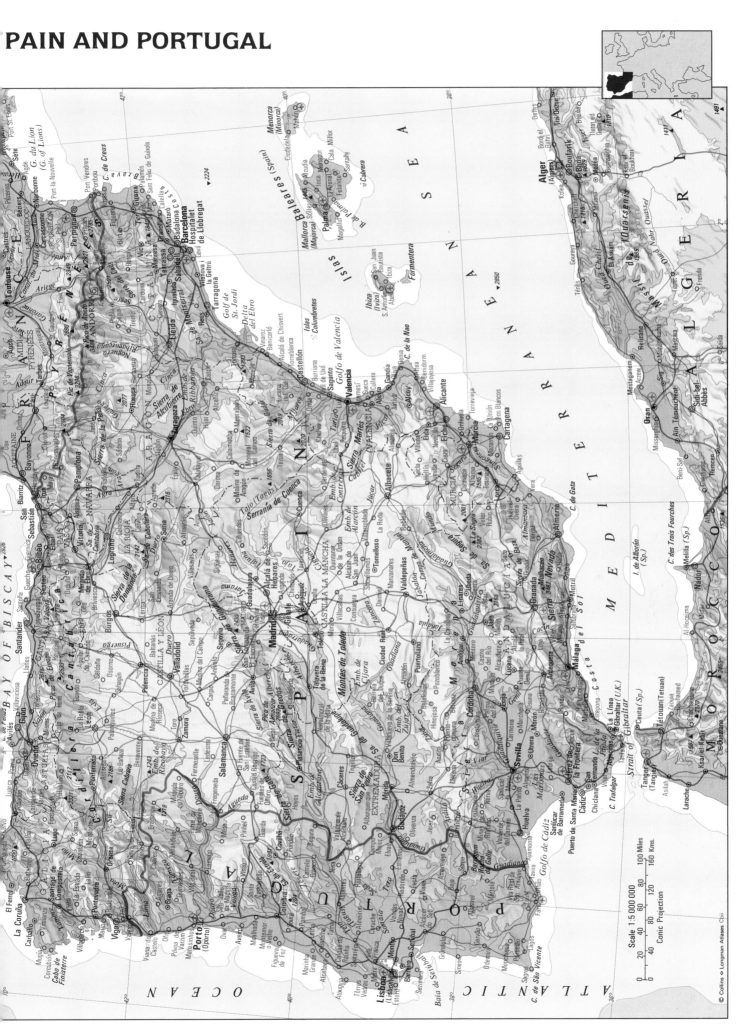

Scale 1:5 000 000
Conic Projection

© Collins ◇ Longman Atlases Cbii

ITALY AND THE BALKANS

CENTRAL EUROPE

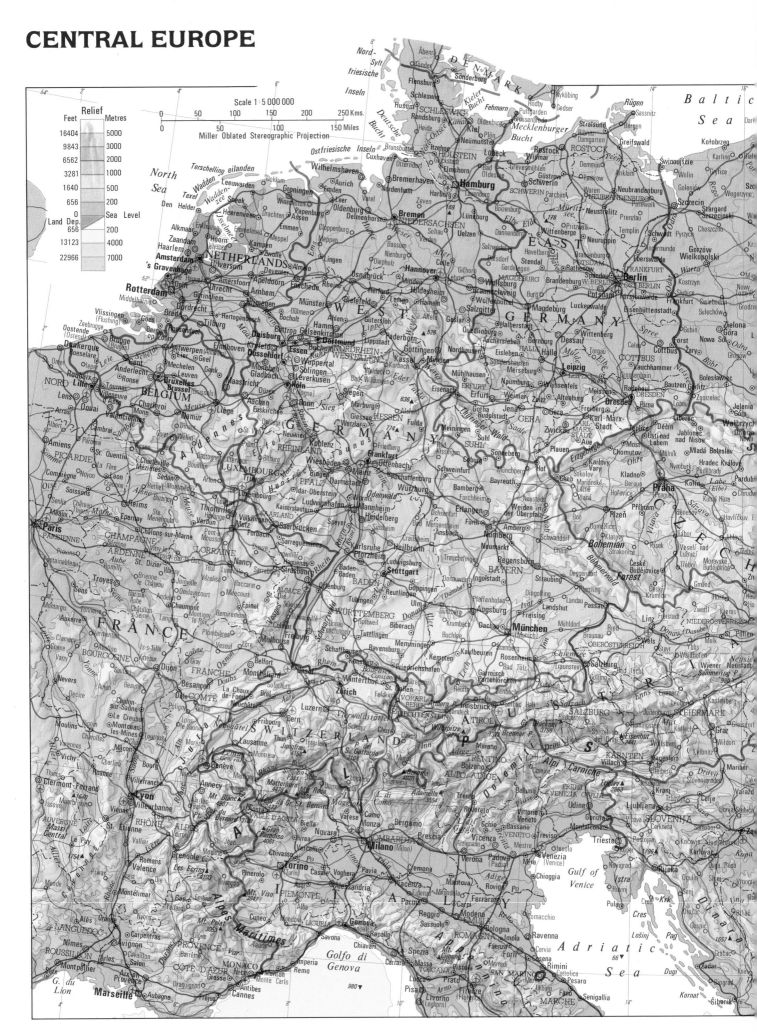

SCANDINAVIA AND BALTIC LANDS

ICELAND
on the same scale

© Wm. Collins Sons & Co. Ltd.

FAROE IS.
on the same scale

Scale 1 : 5 000 000

Conic Projection

100 Miles
160 Kms.

Relief

Feet	Metres
16404	5000
9843	3000
6562	2000
3281	1000
1640	500
656	200
	Sea Level
	Land Dep.
656	200
13123	4000
22966	7000

U.S.S.R. IN EUROPE

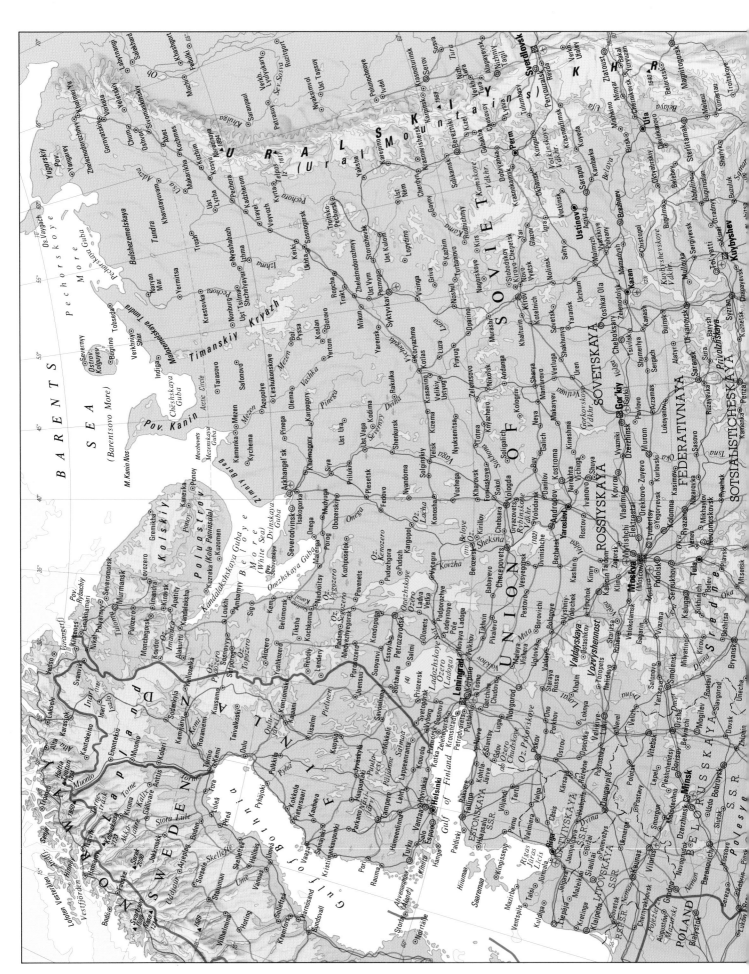

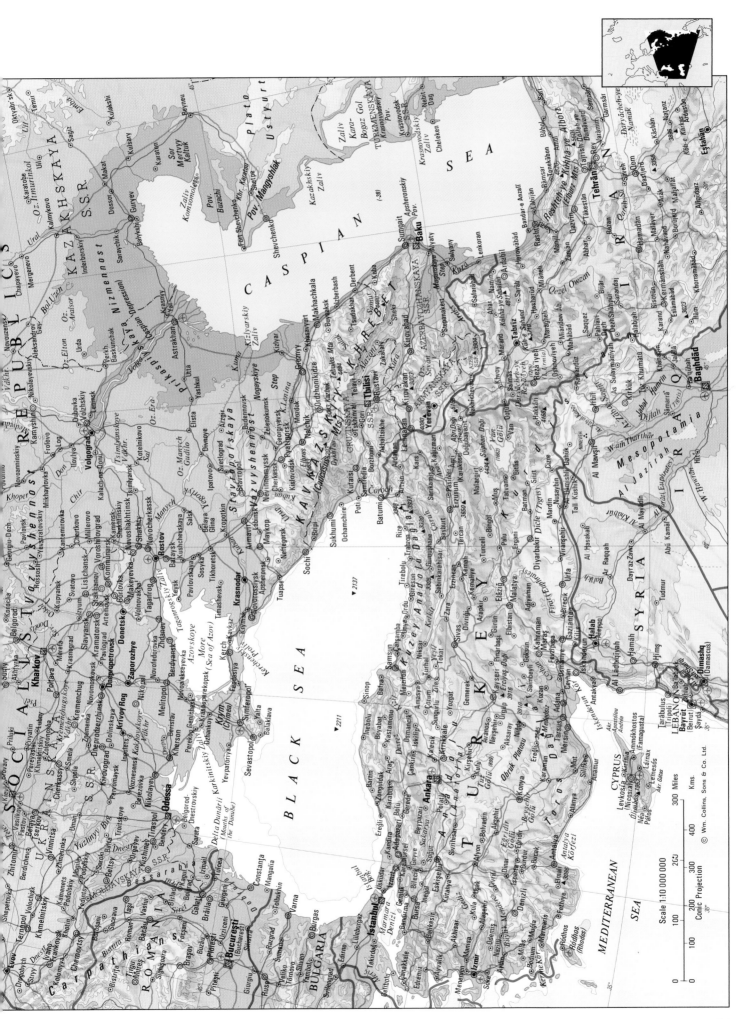

21

U.S.S.R.

Scale 1:20 000 000

| 0 | 100 | 200 | 300 | 400 | 500 Miles |

| 0 | 200 | 400 | 600 | 800 Kms. |

Conic Projection

© Collins · Longman Atlases Ctd

MIDDLE EAST AND SOUTH ASIA

Scale 1 : 20 000 000

0   100   200   300   400   500 Miles

0   200   400   600   800 Kms.

Bonne Projection

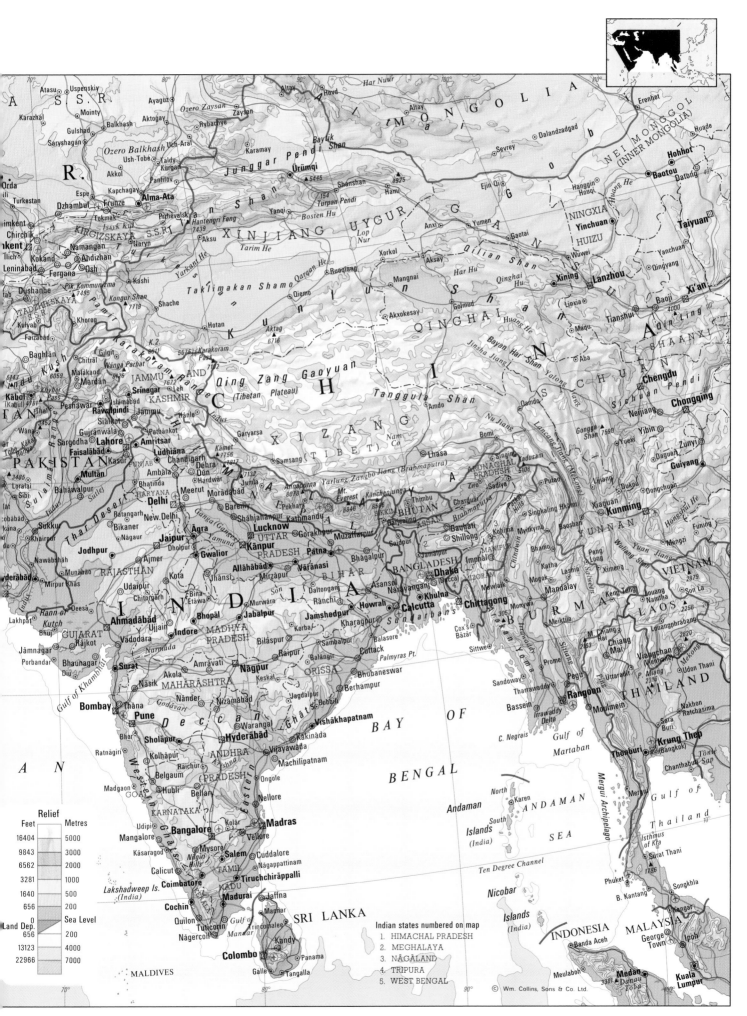

A map of South Asia, East Asia, and Southeast Asia, centered on India and China.

Relief

Feet	Metres
16404	5000
9843	3000
6562	2000
3281	1000
1640	500
656	200
0	Sea Level
Land Dep.	
656	200
13123	4000
22966	7000

Indian states numbered on map
1. HIMACHAL PRADESH
2. MEGHALAYA
3. NĀGĀLAND
4. TRIPURA
5. WEST BENGAL

© Wm. Collins, Sons & Co. Ltd.

FAR EAST AND SOUTHEAST ASIA

Relief

Feet	Metres
16404	5000
9843	3000
6562	2000
3281	1000
1640	500
656	200
	Sea Level
656	200
13123	4000
22966	7000

Land Dep.
0

© Wm. Collins, Sons, & Co. Ltd.

Scale 1:20 000 000

Bonne Projection

| 0 | 100 | 200 | 300 | 400 | 500 Miles |
| 0 | 200 | 400 | 600 | 800 Kms. |

Chinese state numbered on map

1. TIANJIN

PHILIPPINES

Luzon

Manila

Mindanao

SOUTH CHINA SEA

THAILAND

CAMBODIA

MALAYSIA

SINGAPORE
Singapore

BRUNEI

BORNEO

SARAWAK

KALIMANTAN

SABAH

I N D O N E S I A

S U M A T E R A

J A V A (JAWA)

Jakarta
Bandung

Surabaya
Semarang

CELEBES SEA

SULAWESI (CELEBES)

MOLUCCAS

Halmahera

New Guinea

Pegunungan Maoke

A R A F U R A   S E A

A U S T R A L I A

Gulf of Carpentaria

Arnhem Land

Darwin

TIMOR SEA

I N D I A N   O C E A N

Timor

Laut Flores (FLORES SEA)

Nusa Tenggara (Lesser Sunda Islands)

Bali

Flores

Sumba

Sumbawa

Lombok

BELAU

Philippine Trench

10497

Samar

Cebu

Negros

Mindoro

Palawan

SULU SEA

Sandakan

Kota Kinabalu

Banda Aceh

Medan

Padang

Palembang

Bengkulu

Lampung

Java Trench

7450

Christmas I. (Austl.)

Cocos Is. (Austl.)

27

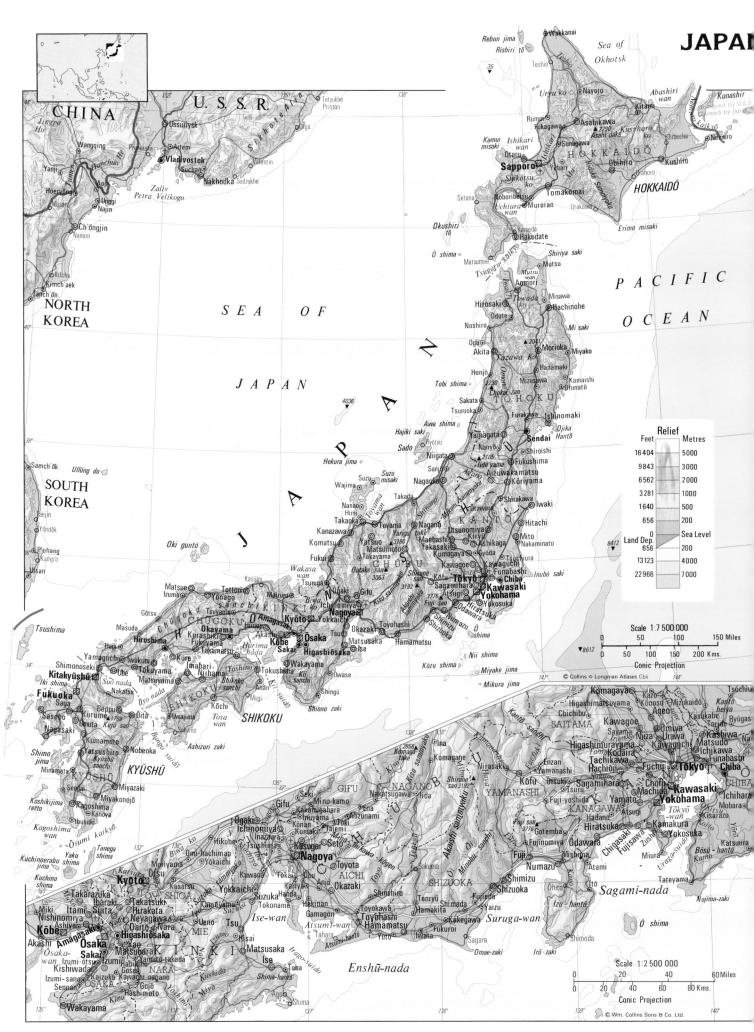

JAPAN

NEW ZEALAND

Relief

Feet	Metres
16 404	5000
9 843	3000
6 562	2000
3 281	1000
1 640	500
656	200
0	Sea Level

Land Dep.	
656	200
13 123	4000
22 966	7000

NORTH ISLAND

SOUTH ISLAND

TASMAN SEA

PACIFIC OCEAN

Scale 1:6 000 000

0   50   100   150 Miles

0   50   100   150   200 Kms.

Conic Projection

© Collins ◇ Longman Atlases Cbii

PACIFIC OCEAN

SAMOA ISLANDS
Scale 1:7 500 000

Falealupo Agee Fagamalo
Salailua Puapua Saleleloga
Savai'i Matautu Upolu
WESTERN Apia Tiavea
SAMOA Samoa Manua Is.
(U.S.A.) Ofu Olosega
Pago Pago Matatula Tau
Tutuila Steps Pt.

FIJI 180°
Gt. Sea Reef Undu C. Vanua Levu
Lambasa Mbutha
Mbua Taveuni
Koro Yathata
Lautoka Viti Koro
Nandi Levu Ngau Sea
Singatoka Suva
Lau
Group
Kandavu Passage
Kandavu
Scale 1:15 000 000

RAROTONGA 159°45'
(N.Z.)
Avatiu Avarua
Pokoinu 438 Matavera
Arorangi Te 653 Ngatangiia
Mangà
Muri
21°15' 21°15'
Tupapa
Titikaveka
Scale 1:500 000 159°45'

NIUE 169°50'
(N.Z.)
Hikutavake Mutalau
Tuapa Toi Lakepa
Makefu Liku
Alofi Motutapu
Bay Alofi
Avatele 66
Avatele
Bay Vaiea
Tepa Pt. Hakupu
Scale 1:1 000 000 169°50'

GUAM 145°
(U.S.A.)
Ritidian
Pt.
Philippine Pati Pt.
Sea Mt. Santa Rosa
13°30' 262 Catalina 13°30'
Agana Pt.
Orote Yona
Pen. Talofofo
Malolos
Merizo Inarajan
Scale 1:2 000 000 145°

VANUATU AND 166°
NEW CALEDONIA
Banks Is.
C. Cumberland C. Quiros
Espíritu Maewo
Santo Oba
Luganville Pentecost I.
16° Coral
Sea Malekula Ambrim
VANUATU Epi Shepherd
Islands
Emae Tongoa
Vila Efate
Eromanga
Récifs Tana
d'Entrecasteaux
Grand Lenakel
Passage
Grand Aneityum
Récif
de
Cook Île
20° Koumac Lifou Îles Loyauté
Kone Houailou (Loyalty Is.)
Île Maré
Nouvelle Bourail Île des
Calédonie Nouméa Pins
(New Caledonia)
(Fr.)
© Wm. Collins Sons & Co. Ltd. 166°
Scale 1:15 000 000

Main map labels

Sea of
Okhotsk
BERING
SEA
Aleutian Basin
Komandorskiye
Ostrova (U.S.S.R.)
Aleutian Islands
Amur
Sakhalin
Kuril'skiye Ostrova
Kuril Ridge
Kuril Trench
Beijing (Peking) Vladivostok
Pyongyang Sapporo
NORTH Hokkaidō
Xi'an KOREA Sea of
(Sian) Sŏul Japan
Qingdao Seoul Honshū
CHINA SOUTH Kōbe JAPAN
Chengdu KOREA Ōsaka Tokyo
Huang H. Shikoku
Chongqing Nanjing Kyūshū
(Chungking) (Nanking) Shanghai
Wuhan East China
Nanchang Sea
Taipei Nansei Shotō
Guangzhou Okinawa Trench
Nanning (Canton) TAIWAN
Beibu HONG KONG
Wan (U.K.)
Hainan
South China
Sea Luzon
Quezon
City Manila
Thanh Pho PHILIPPINES
Ho Chi Minh Palawan
(Ho Chi Minh City)
Sulu
Sea Mindanao
BRUNEI Sulu
Archipelago
Celebes
Sea 5520
Borneo
(Kalimantan)
Selat Makasar
INDONESIA
Laut Jawa (Java Sea)
Jakarta Jawa (Java)
Surabaya Flores
Java Trench Sumba
7450 6218 Timor
Timor
Sea
Darwin
Wyndham Arafura Sea
Broome Gulf
of
Carpentaria
Tennant
Creek
Geraldton AUSTRALIA
Perth Kalgoorlie
Great
Australian Port
Bight Augusta
Albany Adelaide
South Australian Melbourne
Basin

PHILIPPINE
SEA
Mariana
Ridge
Mariana
Islands
Mariana
Trench
Guam (U.S.A.)
Yap
Caroline Hall Is.
Namonuito Truk Is.
Wolear Ponape
Eauripik Pingelap
West Caroline Islands
Caroline Basin East
Caroline Basin
Trust Territory of the Pacific Islands. (U.S.A.)
MICRONESIA
Admiralty Is.
Manus Bismarck
PAPUA Sea New
NEW Ireland
GUINEA New
Puncak Jaya Britain
5030 Bougainville
SOLOMON
ISLANDS
Port Guadalcanal
Moresby Malaita
Torres Strait Santa Cruz
Thursday I. Is.
Coral Sea Basin
Cairns 4715
Great Îles Chesterfield
Barrier (Fr.)
Reef Nouvelle
CORAL Calédonie
SEA (New Caledonia)
(Fr.) Nouméa
Brisbane
Middleton
Reef
Lord Howe I.
Ball's Pyramid
Newcastle Norfolk I.
Sydney (Aus.)
Canberra TASMAN
Murray 128
SEA
King I. Flinders I. Furneaux
Group
Tasmania
Hobart
Bruny I.

BERING
SEA
8100 7429
NORTH
PACIFIC
OCEAN
1962
1634
Midway Is.
(U.S.A.)
Lisianski Laysan
Marcus I.
6148 Wake I.
1477 (U.S.A.)
1440
Johnston I.
(U.S.A.)
Enewetak Bikini
Marshall
Islands
Ralik Chain Ratak Chain
Majuro
Ebon Jaluit
Butaritari
Tarawa
KIRIBATI
NAURU Banaba
(Ocean I.) Kingsmill
Group
TUVALU Nui Vaitupu
Nanumea Funafuti
Phoenix Abariringa
Islands Rawaki
Nikumaroro Orona
WESTERN
SAMOA Atafu Tokelau Is.
Nukunono (N.Z.)
Swains I.
Wallis Apia Manua Is.
(Fr.) Savai'i (U.S.A.)
Upolu Tutuila
Alofi
FIJI Niue
Viti Vanua Levu
Levu Suva Lau
Group TONGA
Nuku'alofa Ha'apai Group
Tongatapu 10882
Group
South
Fiji
Basin
5303
Norfolk Kermadec Raoul
Ridge Trench (N.Z.)
10047
Three Kings Is.
NEW
ZEALAND
Auckland North Island
Wellington
Chatham Rise Chatham Is.
Christchurch
South Island Dunedin
Bluff Bounty Is.
Stewart I.
The Snares
New Zealand Antipodes Is.
Auckland Is. 6098
Plateau
Campbell I.
Macquarie I.
(Aus.)
Indian-Antarctic Ridge
Eastern Indian-
Antarctic Basin Balleny Is.
(N.Z.)

International Date Line

HAWAIIAN ISLANDS
(U.S.A.)

Scale 1:10 000 000

KIRITIMATI (CHRISTMAS I.)
(Kiribati)

Scale 1:2 500 000

TONGA
Scale 1:7 500 000

MARQUESAS ISLANDS
(France)

Íles Marquises
(Marquesas Is.)

Scale 1:10 000 000

EASTER ISLAND
(Chile)

Isla de Pascua
(Easter I.)

Scale 1:1 000 000

SOCIETY ISLANDS
(France)

TAHITI
(France)

Scale 1:2 500 000

Íles de la Société
(Society Islands)

Scale 1:7 500 000

Scale 1:60 000 000

0 200 400 600 800 1000 Miles

0 400 800 1200 1600 Kms.

Modified Zenithal Equidistant Projection

49801

WESTERN AUSTRALIA

Goulburn Is
Croker
Mann
Arnhem Land
Oenpelli
Roper
Roper Valley
Hatches Creek
Mt. Laughlen
Bloods Range
Dundas Str.
Cobourg Pen.
Van Diemen Gulf
Katherine
Mataranka
Larrimah
Daly Waters
Powell Creek
Renner Springs
Barrow Creek
Deep Well
Ewaninga
Finke
Melville I.
Clarence Str.
Pine Creek
Birdum
Sturt Plain
Newcastle Waters
L. Woods
Tennant Creek
Tea Tree
Mt. Freeling 936
Mt. Ziel 1510
Alice Springs
Hugh
Henbury
Bathurst I.
Anson B.
Darwin
Rum Jungle
Batchelor
Burrundie
Daly
Willeroo
Victoria River Downs
Wave Hill
NORTHERN
L. Woods
TERRITORY
Lander
The Granites
Macdonnell Ranges
Palmer
Erldunda
Kulgera
Musgrave Ranges
Mt. Woodroffe 1440
Hamilton
Joseph Bonaparte Gulf
Queens Ch.
Port Keats
Cambridge G.
Ord
Kununurra
Mistake Creek
Inverway
Nicholson
Gordon Downs
Tanami
Sturt Ck.
Gregory L.
L. White
Mackay
Bonython Ra.
L. Macdonald
Hopkins
Petermann Ranges
Barrow Ra.
Tomkinson Ranges
Warburton Ra.
TIMOR SEA
C. Londonderry
Drysdale
Wyndham
Turkey Creek
Kimberley Plateau
Halls Creek
Margaret River
Southesk Tablelands
C. Lévêque
Admiralty G.
Kalumburu
Mt. Hann 776
Gibb River
Glenroy
King Leopold Ranges
Fitzroy Crossing
Jubilee Downs
Christmas Creek
Percival Lakes
L. Disappointment
WESTERN
Gibson Desert
Carnegie
Bonaparte Archipelago
Brunswick B.
Collier B.
Ellendale
Noonkanbah
Derby
Canning Basin
Great Sandy Desert
L. Dora
Carnegie
Granite Peak
Mikiniki
Kupang Timor
Roti
Scott Reef
King Sound
Yeeda River
Fitzroy
Dampier Land
Beagle Bay Mission
Broome
Roebuck B.
La Grange
Anna Plains
Mandora
Wangapuu
Baing
1150
Rowley Shoals
Eighty Mile Beach
Da Grey
Mount Goldsworthy
De Grey
Niningarra
Marble Bar
Nullagine
Balfour Downs
Mount Nicholas
Mundiwindi
Three Rivers
Mooloogool
Wiluna
Sumba
Port Hedland
Roebourne
Wodgina
Marble Bar
Coolawanyah
Wittenoom
Hamersley Range
Mount Newman
Opthalmia Range
Mt. Egerton 994
Robinson Ranges
Peak Hill
Meekatharra
Dampier
Mardie
Onslow
Deepdale
Boolaloo
Ton Price 1227
Ashburton
Mount Vernon
Lyons
Landor
Moorarie
Barrow I.
North West C.
Exmouth
Learmonth
Minderoo
Bullara
Barlee Range
Mt. Augustus 1105
Gascoyne Junction
Murchison
Cardabia
Exmouth Gulf
L. McLeod
Boologooro
Gascoyne
Carnarvon
Wooramel
Geographe Channel
Shark B.
Dirk Hartog
Denham
Tamala
1540
OCEAN
Tropic of Capricorn
Naturaliste Channel

Relief	Metres		Feet
	5000		16404
	3000		9843
	2000		6562
	1000		3281
	500		1640
	200		656
	Sea Level		0
	200	Land Dep.	656
	4000		13123
	7000		22966

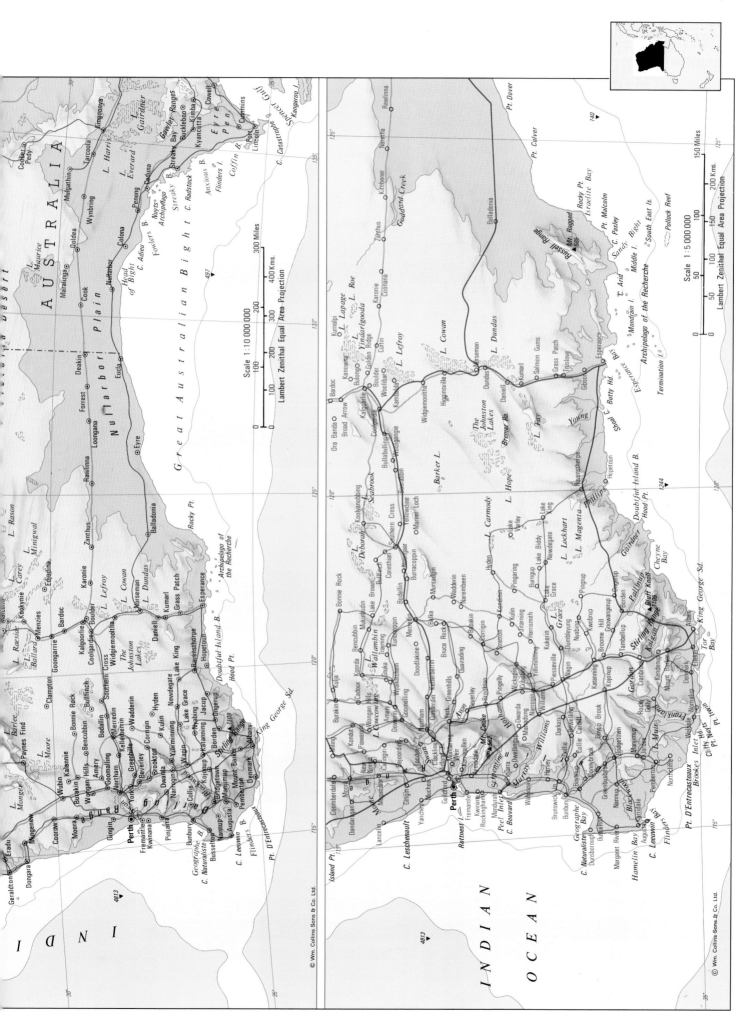

33

EASTERN AUSTRALIA

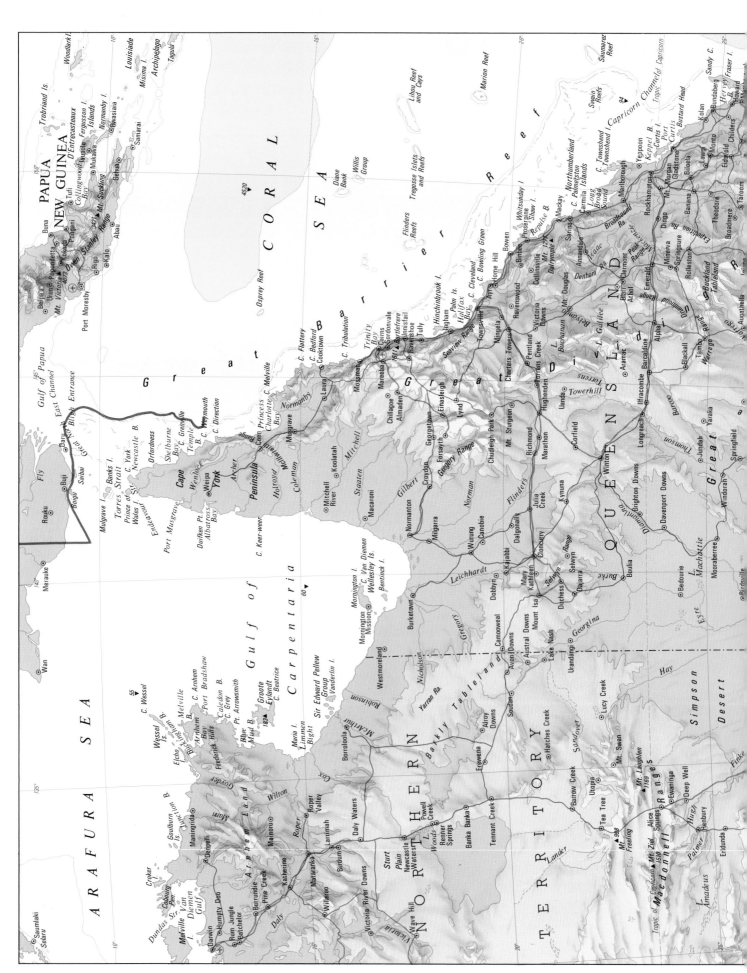

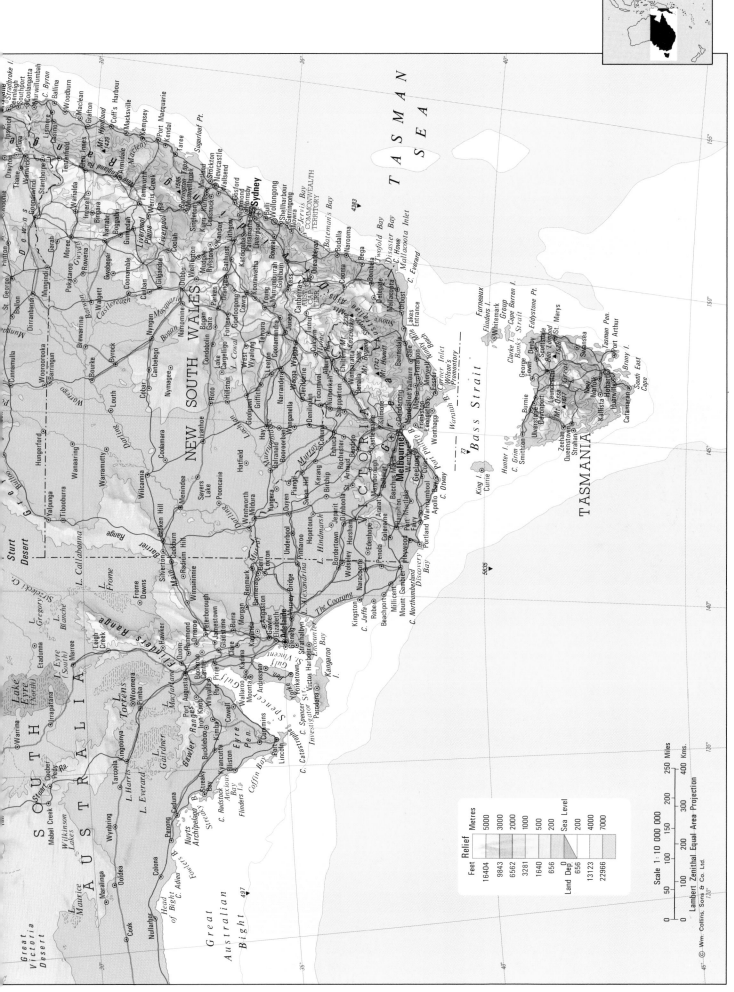

T A S M A N   S E A

NEW SOUTH WALES

Sydney

VICTORIA

Melbourne

SOUTH AUSTRALIA

Adelaide

TASMANIA

Hobart

Bass Strait

Great Australian Bight

Great Victoria Desert

Sturt Desert

Lake Eyre (North)
Lake Eyre (South)

Feet	Relief	Metres
16404		5000
9843		3000
6562		2000
3281		1000
1640		500
656		200
	Sea Level	0
	Land Dep.	656
656		200
13123		4000
22966		7000

Scale 1:10 000 000

0 50 100 200 300 400 Kms.
0 50 100 200 250 Miles

Lambert Zenithal Equal Area Projection

© Wm. Collins, Sons & Co. Ltd.

SOUTHEAST AUSTRALIA

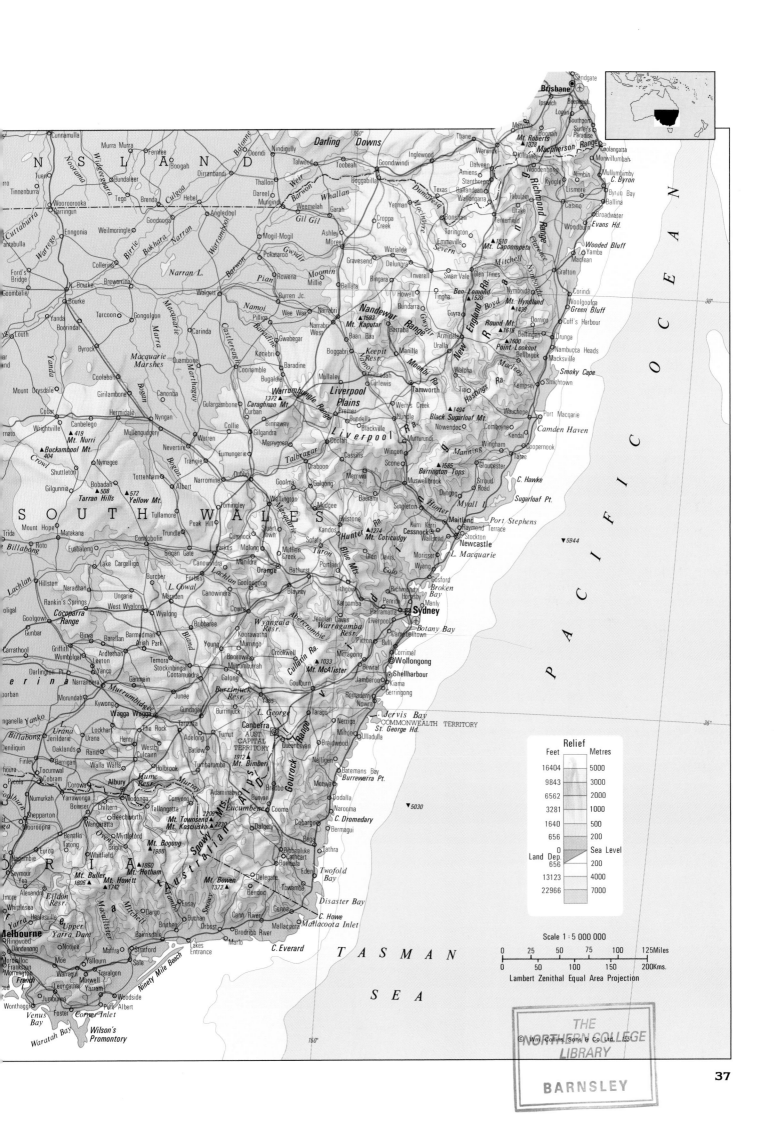

CANADA AND ALASKA

Relief

Feet		Metres
16404		5000
9843		3000
6562		2000
3281		1000
1640		500
656		200
0		Sea Level

Land Dep.

656		200
13123		4000
22966		7000

Scale 1:17 000 000

0	100	200	300	400	500 Miles

| 0 | 100 | 200 | 300 | 400 | 500 | 600 | 700 | 800 Kms. |

Bonne Projection

UNITED STATES

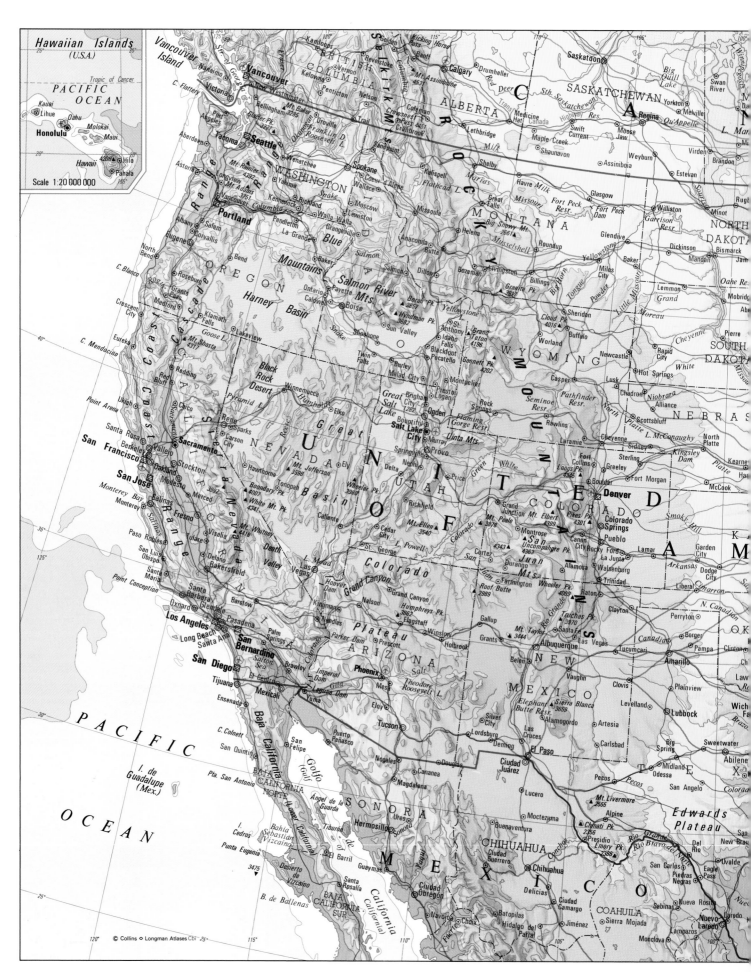

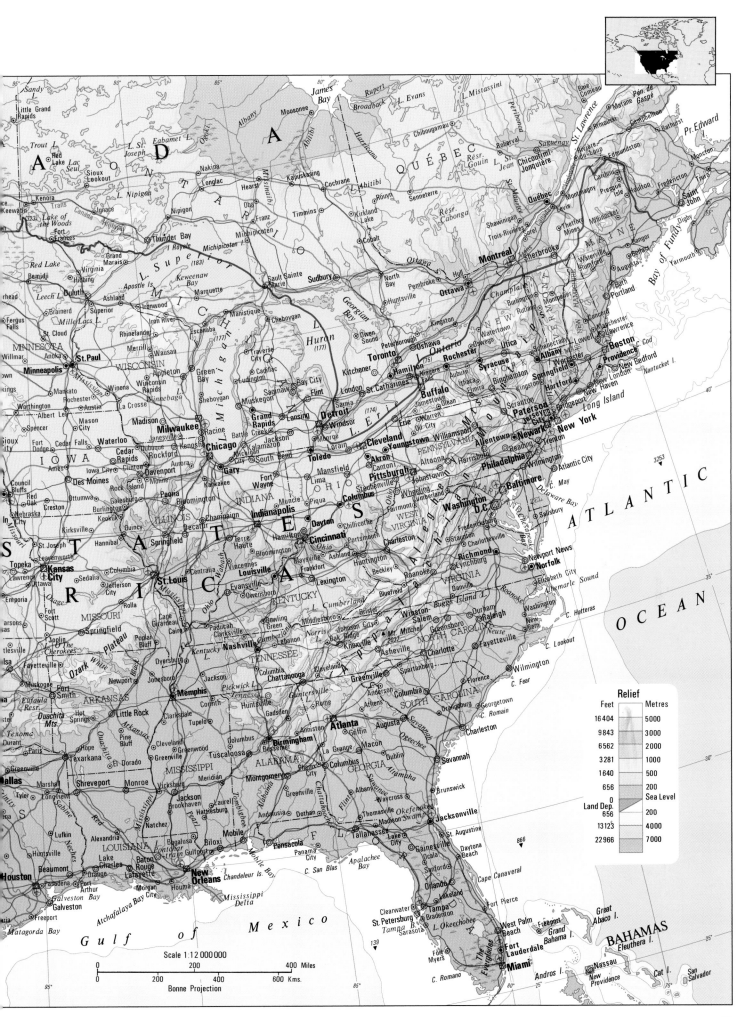

CENTRAL AMERICA AND THE CARIBBEAN

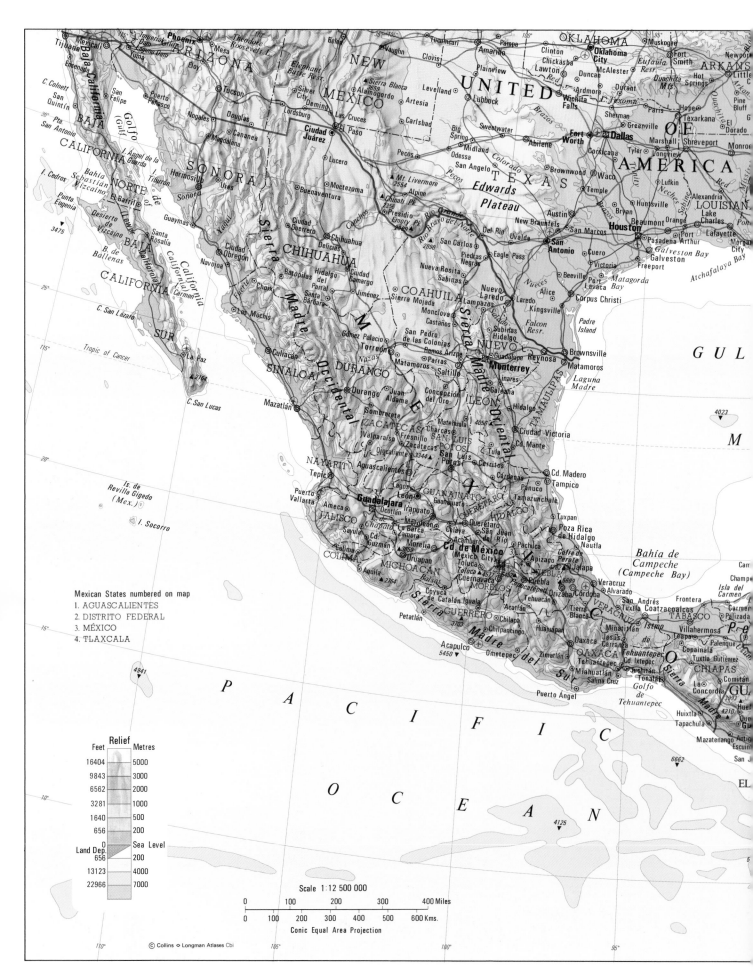

Mexican States numbered on map
1. AGUASCALIENTES
2. DISTRITO FEDERAL
3. MÉXICO
4. TLAXCALA

Relief		
Feet		Metres
16404		5000
9843		3000
6562		2000
3281		1000
1640		500
656		200
0		Sea Level
Land Dep.		
656		200
13123		4000
22966		7000

Scale 1:12 500 000

0   100   200   300   400 Miles

0   100 200 300 400 500 600 Kms.

Conic Equal Area Projection

© Collins ◇ Longman Atlases Cbi

TENNESSEE
Columbia
Asheville
NORTH
C. Lookout
Pickwick L.
Chattanooga
Cleveland
Spartanburg
Charlotte
Fayetteville
New Bern
Huntsville
Guntersville
Anderson
CAROLINA
Tennessee R.
Gadsden
Rome
Athens
SOUTH
Florence
Wilmington
Anniston
Atlanta
Augusta
CAROLINA
Georgetown
Birmingham
Griffin
Savannah R.
C. Romain
ALABAMA
Columbus
GEORGIA
Orangeburg
Charleston
Montgomery
La Grange
Ogeechee
C. Fear
Greenville
Albany
Macon
Savannah
Andalusia
Dublin
Waycross
Brunswick
Pensacola
Dothan
Flint
Altamaha
Panama
Tallahassee
Thomasville
Madison
Brunswick
City
Apalachee
Lake City
ATLANTIC
Mobile Bay
C. San Blas
Bay
Gainesville
Jacksonville
deleur R.
Ocala
St. Augustine
Mississippi
Daytona Beach
OCEAN
Delta
FLORIDA
Sanford
Cape Canaveral
866
Orlando
Clearwater
Lakeland
Fort Pierce
Tampa
St. Petersburg
1137
Tampa B.
Bradenton
West
Great
Tropic of Cancer
Sarasota
Lake
Palm
Freeport
Abaco
Okeechobee
Beach
Grand
Fort Myers
Fort
Bahama I.
OF
The
Lauderdale
Eleuthera I.
Everglades
New
C. Romano
Providence
Rock Sound
Great
C. Sable
Miami
Nicolls
Nassau
Cat I.
San
Town
Salvador
Key West
Andros
The Bight
Florida Keys
Town
Rolleville
Rum Cay
Straits
Andros
Gt.
Samana Cay
Exuma
Long I.
Plana Cays
of
Mayaguana I.
La Habana
Crooked I.
Turks and Caicos Is.
Cárdenas
Archo. de Sabana
Acklin's I.
(U.K.)
Matanzas
Florida
Sagua
Archo. de Camagüey
Caicos Is.
Turks Is.
Marianao
(Havana)
Güines
la Grande
Caibarién
Pinar del Rio
Golfo de
Santa Clara
Great
Matthew
Yucatán
Guane
Batabanó
Cienfuegos
Sancti
Morón
Inagua
Île de
Puerto Plata
8528
Puerto Rico Trench
C. San
Nueva
Spíritus
Ciego de Ávila
la Tortue
San Francisco
San Juan
Tizimín
Antonio
Gerona
Archo. de los
Trinidad
Nuevitas
Holguín
Baracoa
Port-de-Paix
de Macorís
Samaná
Bayamón
G. Catoche
Puerto
Isla de
Canarreos
CUBA
Camagüey
Banes
Cap-Haïtien
Valverde
Arecibo
Juárez
Pinos
Victoria
Bayamo
Gonaïves
Santiago
DOMINICAN
San Juan
Valladolid
las Tunas
S. Luis
Guantánamo
G. de la
St. Marc
La Vega
REP.
Caguas
ax
Isla de
Jardines de la
Manzanillo
Gonâve
S. Pedro
PUERTO
Cozumel
Reina
Sa. Maestra
Santiago
Île de la
HAITI
Azua
de Macorís
Mayagüez
Ponce
QUINTANA
Turquino
de Cuba
Gonâve
Port-au-
S. Cristóbal
La Romana
Mona
RICO
ROO
1974
C. Cruz
2414
Les
Prince
Santo
Saona
(U.S.A.)
Chetumal
Little
Jérémie
Cayes
2680
Domingo
Bay
Cayman
Cayman Brac
Barahona
Corozal
Grand Cayman
Hispaniola
Ambergris
4647
Georgetown
Cayman Is.
Antilles
Cay
(U.K.)
4297
Belize
Montego Bay
St. Ann's Bay
Turneffe Is.
Black River
Port
15°
BELIZE
JAMAICA Kingston
Antonio
Gulf of Honduras
May Pen
Pta.
Is.
Gorda
de la Bahía
Dángriga
C. Camarón
Pto. Cortés
Laguna de
Tela
Balfate
Caratasca
Netherlands
S. Pedro Sula
Trujillo
Antilles
Uluá R.
La Ceiba
Aruba
Curaçao
Bonaire
Sta.
Yoro
Mosquitia
C. Gracias á Dios
Willemstad
Rosa
Juticalpa
HONDURAS
Comayagua
2489
Cord.
Pto. Cabezas
Pta. Gallinas
Tegucigalpa
Costa de Mosquitia
Pen. de la
an Salvador
Danlí
Coco R.
Guajira
Golfo de
S. Vicente
Ocotal
2480
I. de
Castilletes
Venezuela
S. Miguel
Choluteca
Cord. Isabelia
Providencia
Santa
Sa. Nevada de
Maracaibo
G. de Fonseca
Prinzapolca
(Col.)
Marta
Sta. Marta
Chinandega
4780
NICARAGUA
Rio Grande
Barranquilla
5775
Concepción
Valencia
León
Lago de
Estondido
I. de
Cartagena
L. de
Mene Grande
Corinto
Managua
San Andrés
Turbaco
Maracaibo
Jinotepe
Granada
(Col.)
Calamar
San Carlos
Trujillo
Managua
L. de
Bluefields
Arjona
Magangué
VENEZUELA
Rivas
Nicaragua
San Carlos
Plato
Barinas
San Juan del Norte
Sincelejo
Mompós
Cúcuta
C. Sta. Elena
Liberia
COSTA
Cereté
San Jorge
Pamplona
Pen. de
Irazú
Montería
Bucaramanga
Nicoya
San
3432
Golfo de los
Colón
Arauca
C. Blanco
José
RICA
Cartago
Mosquitos
Gatún Lake
Turbo
Pto. Quepos
Chirripó
Puerto Rey
Yanumal
Puntarenas
David
Archo. de
Socorro
COLOMBIA
Pta. S. Pedro
PANAMA
las Perlas
El Real
Golfo
Golfo del
Pen. de Osa
Santiago
Penonomé
de Panamá
Darién
Pta. Burica
Pen. de
Atrato R.
43

Relief

Feet	Metres
16 404	5000
9843	3000
6562	2000
3281	1000
1640	500
656	200
0	Sea Level
Land Dep.	Land Dep.
656	200
13 123	4000
22 966	7000

Scale 1:7 500 000

Conic Equidistant Projection

200 Miles
300 Kms.

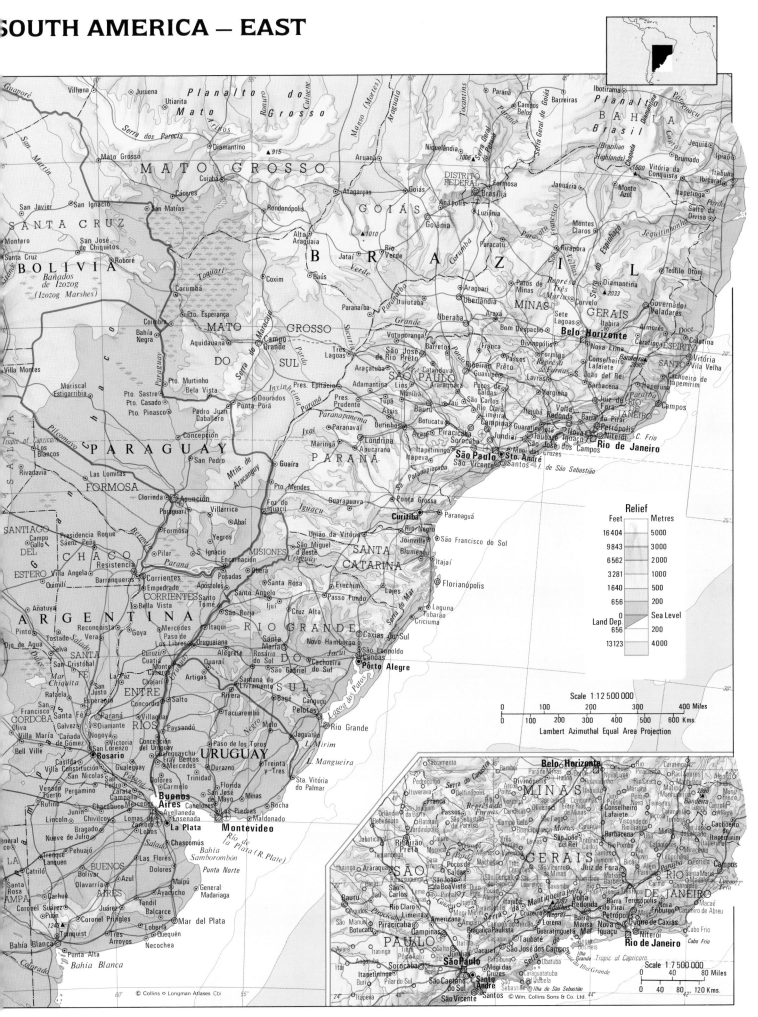

Relief

Feet	Metres
16 404	5000
9843	3000
6562	2000
3281	1000
1640	500
656	200
0	Sea Level
Land Dep.	
656	200
13123	4000

Scale 1:12 500 000

0 100 200 300 400 Miles
0 100 200 300 400 500 600 Kms.

Lambert Azimuthal Equal Area Projection

Scale 1:7 500 000

0   40   80 Miles
0   40   80   120 Kms.

© Collins ○ Longman Atlases Cbi

© Wm. Collins Sons & Co. Ltd.

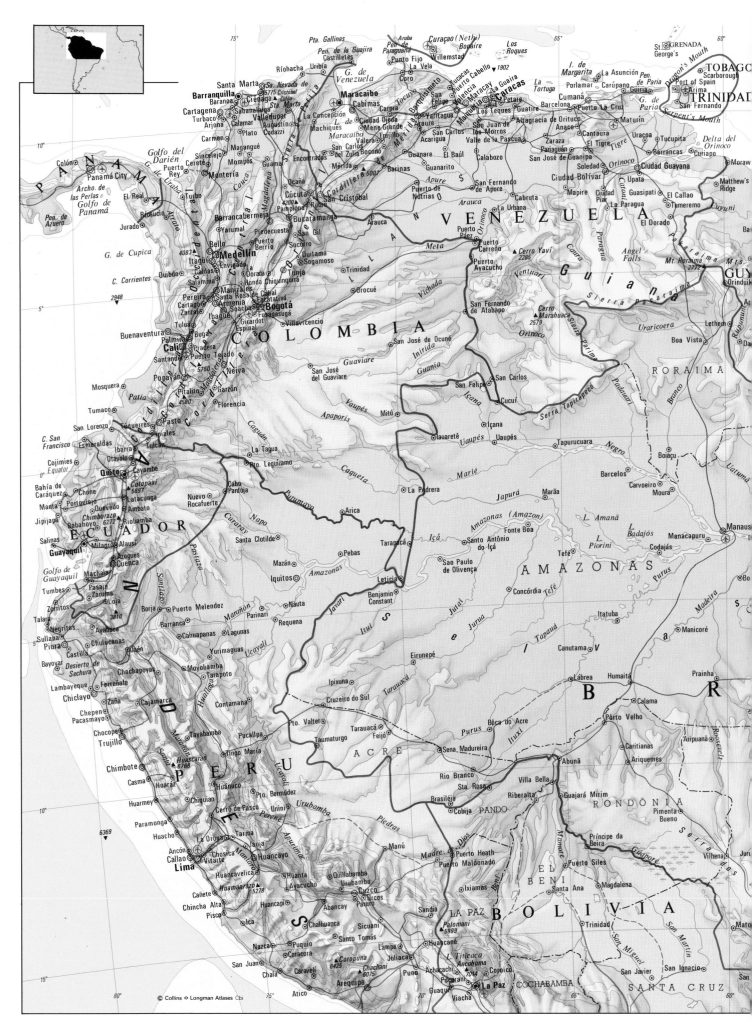

46

Relief

Feet	Metres
16 404	5000
9843	3000
6562	2000
3281	1000
1640	500
656	200
0	Sea Level
Land Dep.	
656	200
13 123	4000

Scale 1:12 500 000

0   100   200   300   400   500 Miles
0 100 200 300 400 500 600 700 800 Kms.

Lambert Azimuthal Equal Area Projection

Amsterdam
Paramaribo
Nieuw Nickerie
Albina
St. Laurent du Maroni
Afobaka
W. J. Van Blommestein Meer
SURINAM
GUIANA (Fr.)
Cayenne
Kaw
C. Orange
St. Georges
Camopi
Oyapock
Tumuc Humac Mts.
Amapá
C. Norte
AMAPÁ
Serra do Navio
Araguari
Merirumã
Pto. Grande
18
Macapá
Mazagão
Estuario do Rio Amazonas (Amazon Delta)
Ilha Caviana
Chaves
I. Grande do Gurupá
I. de Marajó
Salinópolis
Bragança
Capanema
Viseu
Icoraci
Belém
Abaetetuba
Acará
Turiaçu
Cúrurupu
Guimarães
São Luís
Rosário
Tutóia
Parnaíba
Camocim
Granja
Sobral
Antônio Bezerra
Fortaleza
Parangaba
Ipu
Baturité
Aracati
Areia Branca
Macau
Natal
RIO GRANDE DO NORTE
Caicó
Guarabira
João Pessoa
PARAÍBA
Campina Grande
Taipaiana
Itabaiana
Cabedelo
Olinda
Recife
PERNAMBUCO
Caruaru
Belo
Jardim
Palmares
Barreiros
Rio Largo
Maceió
Penedo
ALAGOAS
Arapiraca
SERGIPE
Propriá
Estância
Aracaju
Pedrinhas
Itapicuru
Alagoinhas
Santo Amaro
Salvador
Maragogipe
Nazaré
Valença
Jequié
Ipiaú
Ilhéus
Itabuna
Canavieiras
Salto da Divisa

Óbidos
Prainha
Monte Alegre
Gurupá
Pôrto de Moz
Amazonas (Amazon)
Juruti
Parintins
Santarém
Belterra
Altamira
PARA
Itaituba
Bacabal
Tapajós
Iriri
Jamanxim
Xingu
Irirí
Curuá
Tocantins
Fresco
São Manuel
Jatobá
Marabá
Itacajuna
Tucuruí
Tocantinópolis
Pôrto Franco
Carolina
Riachão
Imperatriz
Barra do Corda
MARANHÃO
Colinas
Teresina
Amarante
Floriano
Oeiras
Uruçui
Picos
PIAUÍ
Paulistana
São João do Piauí
Grajaú
Bacabal
Pedreiras
Codó
Caxias
União
Campo Maior
Crateús
Senador Pompeu
Iguatu
Souza
Pombal
Patos
Cajázeiras
Juàzeiro do Norte
Crato
Serra Talhada
Salgueiro
Arcoverde
Garanhuns
Palmeira dos Índios
Viçosa

Meia
Poti
Itaim
Piauí
Gurguéia
Gurguéia
Paragua
Casa Nova
Petrolina
Juàzeiro
Paulo Afonso
São Francisco
Propriá
Remanso
Parnaguá
Xique Xique
Senhor do Bonfim
Jacobina
Queimadas
Serrinha
Feira de Santana
Cachoeira

BRASIL
Conceição do Araguaia
Araguacema
Araguaia
Sta. Filomena
Pedro Afonso
Chapada das Mangabeiras
884
Barreiras
Ibotirama
Barra
BAHIA
Carinhanha
Brumado
Vitória da Conquista
Ibicaraí
Itapetinga

Pouso Alegre
Serra Formosa
Ronuro
Ilha do Bananal
Peixe
Paranã
Campos Belos
Planalto
Posse
Januária
Monte Azul

MATO GROSSO
Planalto do
Mato Grosso
Diamantino
915
Aruanã
Uruaçu
Niquelândia
1006
Goiás
GOIÁS
DIST. FED.
Brasília
Formosa
MINAS GERAIS
Anápolis
Luziânia
Goiânia
Cuiabá
Aragarças
Rondonópolis
Alto Araguaia

Serra Geral do Paraná
Serra Geral de Goiás
Serra Talhada
Chapada Diamantina
Paraguaçu
Serra da Ibiapaba
Corrente
Brazilian Highlands

Equator

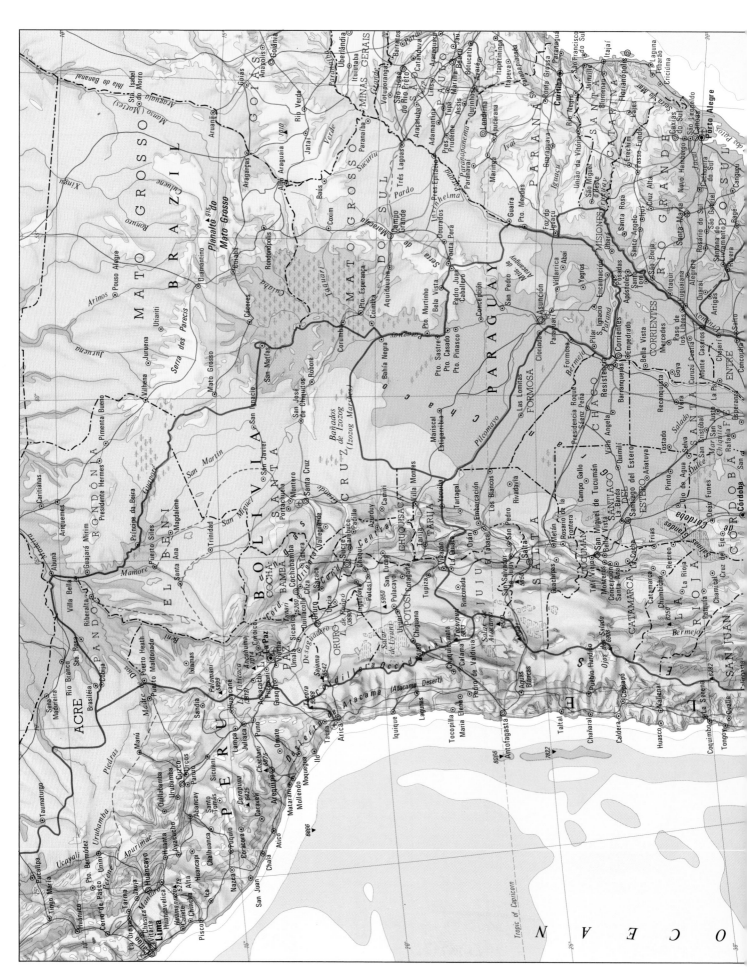

SOUTH

ATLANTIC

OCEAN

PACIFIC

Buenos Aires
Montevideo
Río de la Plata (R. Plate)

ARGENTINA

CHILE

MENDOZA
SAN LUIS
LA PAMPA
RIO NEGRO
NEUQUEN
CHUBUT
SANTA CRUZ

Bahía Blanca
Carmen de Patagones
Golfo San Matías
Pen. Valdés
Punta Delgada
Golfo Nuevo
Rawson
Puerto Madryn
Trelew
C. Dos Bahías
Camarones
Golfo San Jorge
Comodoro Rivadavia
C. Blanco
Deseado
Mazarredo
Bahía Laura
Pto. Santa Cruz
Río Gallegos
Bahía Grande
Pta. Arenas

TIERRA DEL FUEGO
Cabo de Hornos (Cape Horn)

Falkland Is. (U.K.)
West Falkland
East Falkland
Stanley

BRAZIL
URUGUAY
Montevideo

CORRIENTES
ENTRE RIOS
SANTA FE

Rosario
Buenos Aires
BUENOS AIRES

Scale 1 : 7 500 000
0   40   80   Miles
0   40   80   120   Kms.

Relief

Feet	Metres			
16404	5000			
9843	3000			
6562	2000			
3281	1000			
1640	500			
656	200			
0	Sea Level	0		
656	Land Dep.	200		
13123	4000			
22966	7000			

Scale 1 : 12 500 000

0   100   200   300   400 Miles
0   200   400   600 Kns.

Lambert Azimuthal Equal Area Projection

© Collins © Longman Atlases Cbi-55

Wm. Collins Sons & Co. Ltd

NORTHERN AFRICA

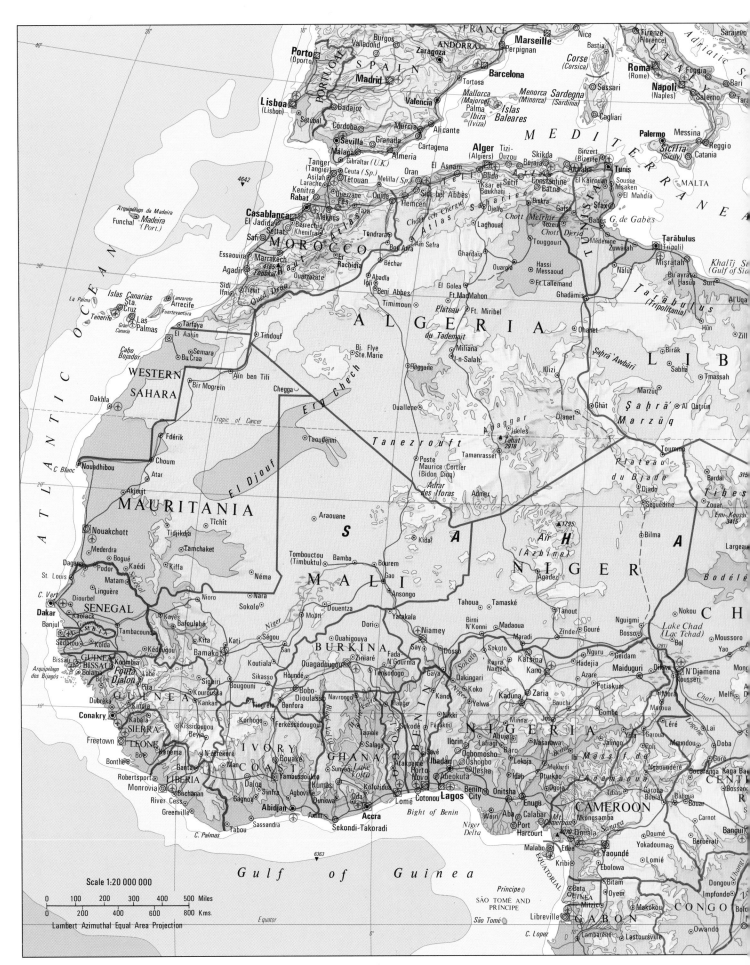

Scale 1:20 000 000

| | 0 | 100 | 200 | 300 | 400 | 500 Miles |
| 0 | 200 | 400 | 600 | 800 Kms. |

Lambert Azimuthal Equal Area Projection

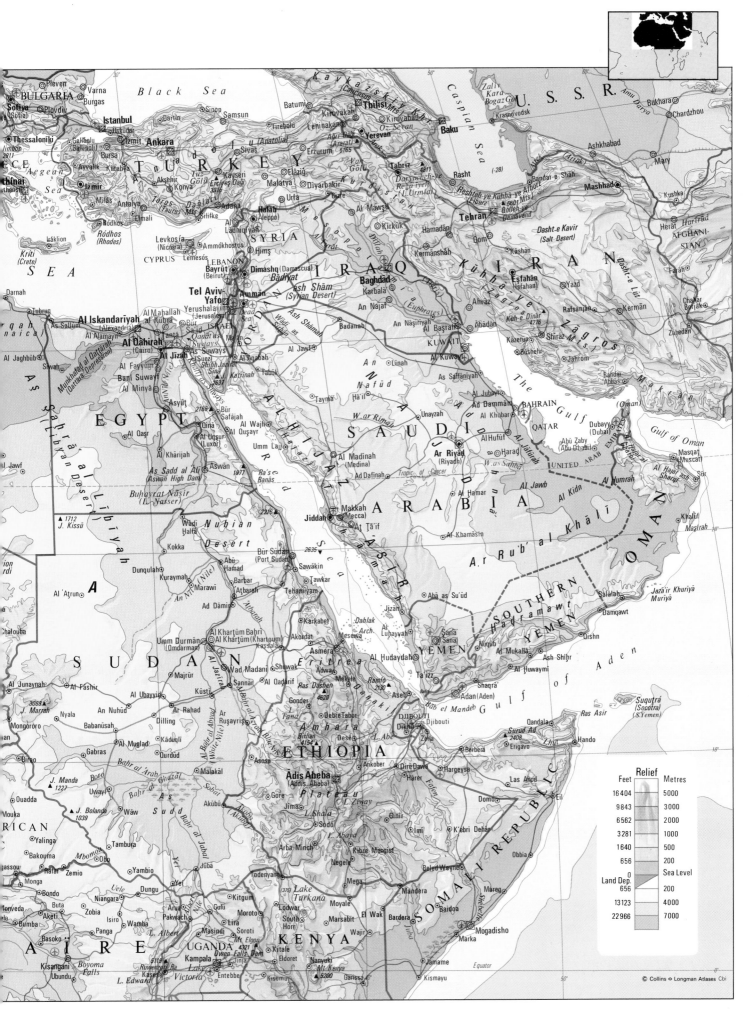

CENTRAL AND EAST AFRICA

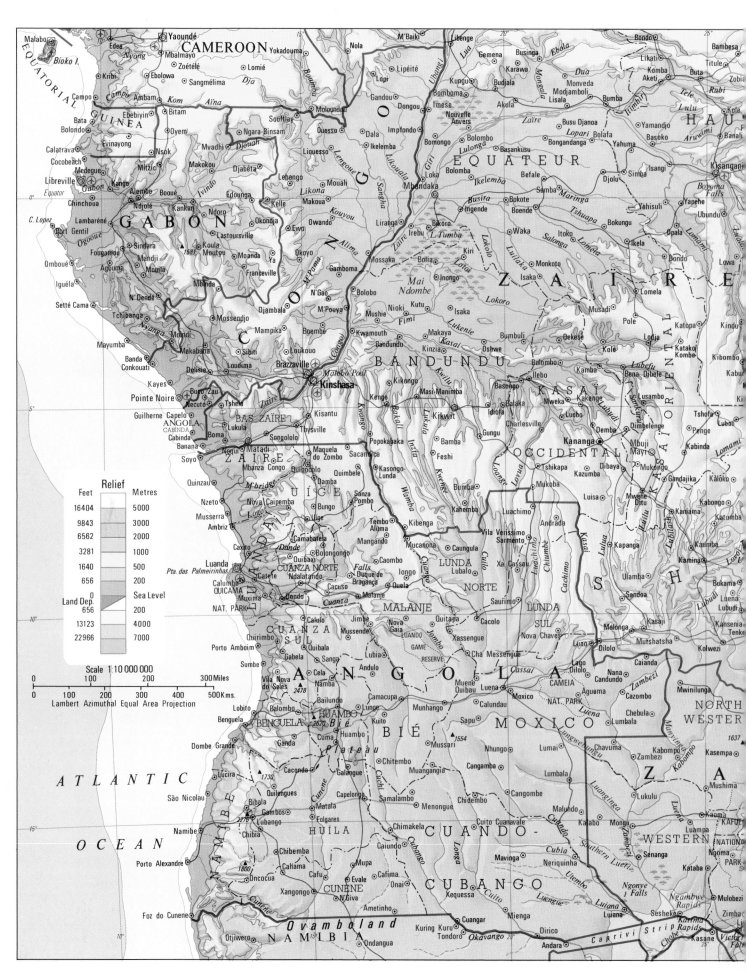

Relief

Feet		Metres
16404		5000
9843		3000
6562		2000
3281		1000
1640		500
656		200
0		Sea Level
Land Dep.		
656		200
13123		4000
22966		7000

Scale 1:10 000 000

Lambert Azimuthal Equal Area Projection

Relief

Metres	Feet
5000	16404
3000	9843
2000	6562
1000	3281
500	1640
200	656
Sea Level	0
200	656 Land Dep.
4000	13123
7000	22966

Scale 1:10 000 000

Lambert Azimuthal Equal Area Projection

300 Miles   500 Kms.

ZIMBABWE

MOZAMBIQUE

BOTSWANA

NAMIBIA

NAMIB DESERT

KALAHARI DESERT

REPUBLIC OF SOUTH AFRICA

TRANSVAAL

ORANGE FREE STATE

CAPE PROVINCE

NATAL

SWAZILAND

LESOTHO

Transkei

Pretoria

Johannesburg

Soweto

Cape Town

Durban

Maputo

Harare

Bulawayo

Windhoek

Walvis Bay

Lake Kariba

Etosha Pan

Okavango Basin

Great Karoo

Little Karoo

Cape of Good Hope

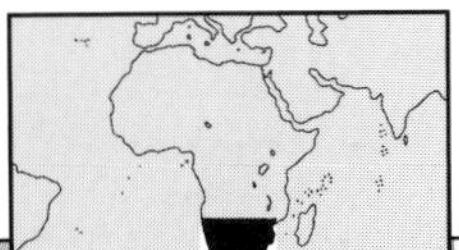

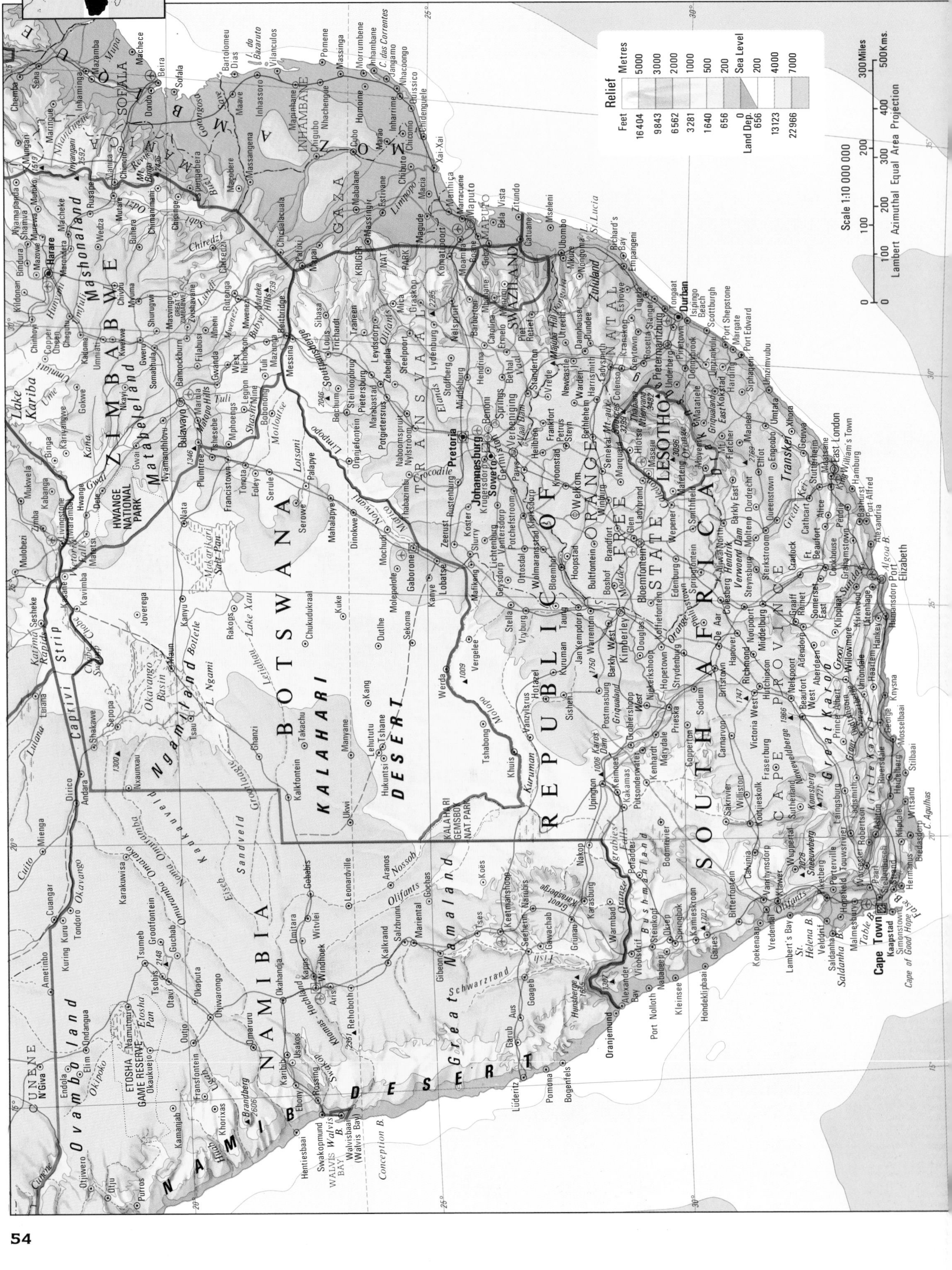

ntroduction

he Index includes an alphabetical list of selected names ppearing on the maps. Each entry consists of the name ollowed by a page reference and the name's location on e map, given by latitude and longitude co-ordinates. ost features are indexed to the largest scale map on hich they appear, however when the name applies to ountries or other extensive features it is generally ndexed to the map on which it appears in its entirety. erial features are generally indexed using co-ordinates which indicate the centre of the feature. The latitude and longitude indicated for a point feature gives the location of the point on the map. In the case of rivers the mouth or confluence is always taken as the point of reference.

Names in the Index are generally in the local language and where a conventional English version exists, this is cross referenced to the entry in the local language. Names of features which extend across the boundaries of more than one country are usually named in English if no single official name exists. Names in languages not written in the Roman alphabet have been transliterated using the official system of the country if one exists, e.g. Pinyin system for China, otherwise the systems recognised by the United States Board on Geographical Names have been used.

Names abbreviated on the maps are given in full in the Index.

bbreviations of Geographical Terms

., B.	bay, Bay	**f.**	physical feature e.g. valley, plain, geographic district or region	**mts., Mts.**	mountains, Mountains
., C.	cape, Cape	**g., G.**	gulf, Gulf	**pen., Pen.**	peninsula, Peninsula
.	internal division e.g. county, region, state.	**i., I., is., Is.**	island, Island, islands, Islands	**Pt.**	Point
es.	desert	**l., L.**	lake, Lake	**r.**	river
st.	estuary	**mtn., Mtn.**	mountain, Mountain	**resr., Resr.**	reservoir, Reservoir
				Sd.	Sound
				str., Str.	strait, Strait

A

achen 16 50.46N 6.06E
arau 16 47.24N 8.04E
are r. 16 47.37N 8.13E
ba 50 5.06N 7.21E
bā as Su'ūd 24 17.28N 44.06E
bādān 24 30.21N 48.15E
badla 50 31.01N 2.45W
bakan 23 53.43N 91.25E
baya, L. 51 6.20N 38.00E
bbeville 12 50.06N 1.51E
bbotsbury 9 50.40N 2.36W
be, L. 51 11.06N 41.50E
béché 51 13.49N 20.49E
benrå 19 55.02N 9.26E
berayron 9 52.15N 4.16W
berdare 9 51.43N 3.27W
berdare Range mts. 53 0.20S 36.40E
berdeen 11 57.08N 2.07W
berdovey 9 52.33N 4.03W
berfeldy 11 56.37N 3.54W
bergavenny 9 51.49N 3.01W
bersoch 8 52.50N 4.31W
berystwyth 9 52.25N 4.06W
bidjan 50 5.19N 4.01W
bilene Tex. 40 32.27N 99.45W
bingdon 9 51.40N 1.17W
bitibi r. 44 51.03N 80.55W
bitibi, L. 44 48.42N 79.45W
bou Deïa 50 11.20N 19.20E
boyne 11 57.05N 2.48W
brantes 13 39.28N 8.12W
bruzzi d. 14 42.05N 13.45E
bu Dhabi see Abū Ẓaby 24
bū Ḩamad 51 19.32N 33.20E
buja 50 9.12N 7.11E
bunã 46 9.41S 65.20W
bū Ẓaby 24 24.27N 54.23E
by 19 58.40N 16.11E
byaḑ, Al Baḩr al r. 24 15.38N 32.31E
cámbaro 42 20.01N101.42W
capulco 42 16.51N 99.56W
catlán 42 18.12N 98.02W
ccra 50 5.33N 0.15W
ccrington 8 53.46N 2.22W
chill I. 10 53.57N 10.00W
chinsk 22 56.10N 90.10E
concagua mtn. 48 32.39S 70.00W
cqui 14 44.41N 8.28E
craman, L. 36 32.02S135.26E
damaoua, Massif de l' mts. 50 7.05N 12.00E
Adams N.Y. 44 43.49N 76.01W
dams, Mt. 40 46.13N121.29W
Adan 24 12.50N 45.00E
Adana 21 37.00N 35.19E
Adapazari 21 40.45N 30.23E
Adda r. 14 45.08N 9.55E
Ad Dafīnah 24 23.18N 41.58E
Ad Dāmir 51 17.37N 33.59E
Ad Dammām 24 26.23N 50.08E
Ad Darb 24 17.44N 42.15E
Ad Dawḩah 24 25.15N 51.34E
Addis Ababa see Ādīs Ābeba 51
Adelaide 36 34.56S138.36E
Aden see 'Adan 24
Aden, G. of 24 13.00N 50.00E
Adendorp 54 32.18S 24.31E
Adige r. 14 45.10N 12.20E
Adirondack Mts. 44 44.00N 74.00W
Ādīs Ābeba 51 9.03N 38.42E
Adiyaman 21 37.46N 38.15E
Admiralty Is. 30 2.10S147.00E
Adour r. 12 43.28N 1.35W
Adra 13 36.43N 3.03W
Adrano 14 37.39N 14.49E
Adriatic Sea 14 42.30N 16.00E
Ādwa 51 14.12N 38.56E
Aegean Sea 15 39.00N 25.00E
Afghanistan 25 32.45N 65.00E
Afmadu 53 0.27N 42.05E
Afyon 21 38.46N 30.32E
Agadez 50 17.00N 7.56E
Agadir 50 30.26N 9.36W
Agana 30 13.28N144.45E
Agboville 50 5.55N 4.15W
Agde 12 43.19N 3.28E
Agen 12 44.12N 0.38E
Aghada 10 51.50N 8.13W
Āgra 25 27.11N 78.01E
Agra r. 13 42.12N 1.43W
Agreda 13 41.51N 1.55W
Agri r. 15 40.13N 16.45E
Ağri 21 39.44N 43.03E
Ağri Daği mtn. 21 39.45N 44.15E
Agrigento 14 37.19N 13.36E
Aguascalientes 42 21.51N102.18W
Águeda r. 13 41.00N 6.56W
Aguilas 13 37.25N 1.35W
Agulhas, C. 54 34.50S 20.00E
Agulhas Negras mtn. 45 22.20S 44.43W
Ahaggar mts. 50 24.00N 5.50E
Ahaura 29 42.21S171.33E
Ahlen 16 51.46N 7.53E
Ahmadābād 25 23.02N 72.37E
Ahvāz 24 31.17N 48.44E
Aigues-Mortes 12 43.34N 4.11E
Ailsa Craig i. 11 55.15N 5.07W
Ain r. 12 45.47N 5.12E
Aïna r. 52 0.38N 12.47E
Aïn ben Tili 50 26.00N 9.32W
Aïn Sefra 50 32.45N 0.35W
Aïr mts. 50 18.30N 8.30E
Airdrie 11 55.52N 3.59W
Aire 12 43.39N 0.15W
Aire r. 8 53.42N 0.54W
Aisne r. 12 49.27N 2.55E
Aix-en-Provence 12 43.31N 5.27E
Aix-les-Bains 12 45.42N 5.55E
Aíyina i. 15 37.43N 23.30E
Aíyion 15 38.15N 22.05E
Ajaccio 12 41.55N 8.43E
Ajmer 25 26.27N 74.38E
Akashi 28 34.38N134.59E
Aketi 52 2.46N 23.51E
Akhḑar, Al Jabal al mts. 51 32.10N 22.00E
Akhelóös 15 38.20N 21.04E
Akhisar 15 38.54N 27.49E
Akita 26 39.44N140.05E
Akjoujt 50 19.45N 14.23W
Aklavik 38 68.12N135.00W
Ākobo r. 51 8.30N 33.15E
Akola 25 20.44N 77.00E
Akpatok I. 39 60.30N 68.30W
Akron Ohio 44 41.04N 81.31W
Aksaray 21 38.22N 34.02E
Akşehir 21 38.22N 31.24E
Aksu 25 42.10N 80.00E
Aktogay 22 46.57N 79.40E
Akūbū r. see Ākobo r. 51
Akxokesay 25 36.48N 91.06E
Alabama d. 41 33.00N 87.00W
Alabama r. 41 31.05N 87.55W
Alakurtti 20 67.00N 30.23E
Al 'Alamayn 51 30.50N 28.57E
Alamosa 40 37.28N105.54W
Alanya 21 36.32N 32.02E
Al' Aqabah 24 29.32N 35.00E
Alaşehir 15 38.22N 28.29E
Alaska d. 38 65.00N153.00W
Alaska, G. of 38 58.45N145.00W
Alaska Range mts. 38 62.10N152.00W
Al 'Aţrun 51 18.11N 26.36E
Alazani r. 21 41.06N 46.40E
Alba 14 44.42N 8.02E
Albacete 13 39.00N 1.52W
Alba-Iulia 17 46.04N 23.33E
Albania 15 41.00N 20.00E
Albany r. 39 52.10N 82.00W
Albany Ga. 41 31.37N 84.10W
Albany N.Y. 44 42.39N 73.45W
Albany Oreg. 40 44.38N123.07W
Al Başrah 24 30.33N 47.50E
Al Bayḑā' 51 32.50N 21.50E
Albemarle Sd. 41 36.10N 76.00W
Alberche r. 13 40.00N 4.45W
Albert, L. 53 1.45N 31.00E
Alberta d. 38 55.00N115.00W
Albert Nile r. 53 3.30N 32.00E
Albi 12 43.56N 2.08E
Ålborg 19 57.03N 9.56E
Alborz, Reshteh-ye Kūhhā-ye mts. 24 36.00N 52.30E
Albuquerque 40 35.05N106.38W
Alburquerque 13 39.13N 6.59W
Albury 37 36.03S146.53E
Alcácer do Sal 13 38.22N 8.30W
Alcamo 14 37.59N 12.58E
Alcañiz 13 41.03N 0.09W
Alcaudete 13 37.35N 4.05W
Alcázar de San Juan 13 39.24N 3.12W
Alcira 13 39.10N 0.27W
Alcoy 13 38.42N 0.29W
Alcudia 13 39.51N 3.09E
Aldan 23 58.44N125.22E
Aldan r. 23 63.30N130.00E
Aldeburgh 9 52.09N 1.35E
Alderney i. 9 49.42N 2.11W
Aldershot 9 51.15N 0.47W
Aldridge 9 52.36N 1.55W
Alegrete 49 29.46S 55.46W
Aleksandrovsk Sakhalinskiy 23 50.55N142.12E
Alençon 12 48.25N 0.05E
Aleppo see Ḩalab 24
Alès 12 44.08N 4.05E
Alessandria 14 44.54N 8.37E
Ålesund 18 62.28N 6.11E
Aleutian Is 30 52.00N176.00W
Aleutian Range mts. 38 58.00N156.00W
Alexander Archipelago is. 38 56.30N134.30W
Alexander Bay town 54 28.36S 16.26E
Alexandria B.C. 38 52.38N122.27W
Alexandria Ont. 44 45.18N 74.39W
Alexandria see Al Iskandarīyah 51
Alexandria Va. 44 38.48N 77.03W
Alexandroúpolis 15 40.50N 25.53E
Al Fāshir 51 13.37N 25.22E
Al Fayyūm 51 29.19N 30.50E
Alfiós r. 15 37.37N 21.27E
Alford 11 57.14N 2.42W
Al Furāt r. 24 31.00N 47.27E
Algeciras 13 36.08N 5.27W
Alger 50 36.50N 3.00E
Algeria 50 28.00N 2.00E
Alghero 14 40.33N 8.20E
Algiers see Alger 50
Algoa B. 54 33.50S 26.00E
Al Ḩajar ash Sharqī mts. 51 23.00N 59.00E
Al Ḩamar 24 22.26N 46.12E
Al Ḩudaydah 24 14.50N 42.58E
Al Hufūf 24 25.20N 49.34E
Al Ḩuwaymī 24 14.05N 47.44E
Aliákmon r. 15 40.30N 22.38E
Alicante 13 38.21N 0.29W
Alice Springs town 34 23.42S133.52E
Alima r. 52 1.36S 16.35E
Alingsås 19 57.56N 12.31E
Al Iskandarīyah 51 31.13N 29.55E
Aliwal North 54 30.41S 26.41E
Al Jaghbūb 51 29.42N 24.38E
Al Jawb f. 24 23.00N 50.00E
Al Jawf 24 29.49N 39.52E
Al Jazīrah f. 51 14.30N 33.00E
Al Jīzah 51 30.01N 31.12E
Al Jubayl 24 27.59N 49.40E
Al Junaynah 51 13.27N 22.30E
Al Khābūrah 24 23.58N 57.10E
Al Khamāsīn 24 20.29N 44.49E
Al Khārijah 51 25.27N 30.32E
Al Kharţūm 51 15.33N 32.35E
Al Kharţūm Baḩrī 51 15.39N 32.34E
Al Khubar 51 26.18N 50.06E
Al Kidn des. 24 22.20N 54.20E
Alkmaar 16 52.37N 4.44E
Al Kuwayt 24 29.20N 48.00E
Allāhābād 25 25.27N 81.51E
Allakaket 38 66.30N152.45W
Allegheny r. 44 40.27N 80.00W
Allegheny Mts. 41 38.30N 80.00W
Allen, Lough 10 54.07N 8.04W
Allentown 44 40.37N 75.30W
Aller r. 16 52.57N 9.11E
Alliance Nebr. 40 42.08N103.00W
Allier r. 12 46.58N 3.04E
Alloa 11 56.07N 3.49W
Al Luḩayyah 51 15.43N 42.42E
Alma-Ata 22 43.19N 76.55E
Almaden 34 17.20S144.41E
Almadén 13 38.47N 4.50W
Al Madīnah 24 24.30N 39.35E
Al Manāmah 24 26.12N 50.36E
Almansa 13 38.52N 1.06W
Almanzora r. 13 37.16N 1.49W
Al Mawşil 24 36.21N 43.08E
Almazán 13 41.29N 2.31W
Almeirim 13 39.12N 8.37W
Almelo 16 52.21N 6.40E
Almería 13 36.50N 2.26W
Älmhult 19 56.33N 14.08E
Al Minyā 51 28.06N 30.45E
Al Muglad 51 11.01N 27.50E
Al Mukallā 24 14.34N 49.09E
Al Mukhā 24 13.19N 43.15E
Almuñécar 13 36.44N 3.41W
Alnwick 8 55.25N 1.41W
Alofi 30 19.03S169.55W
Alónnisos i. 15 39.08N 23.50E
Alpes Maritimes mts. 12 44.07N 7.08E
Alpine 40 30.22N103.40W
Alps mts. 12 46.00N 7.30E
Al Qaḑārif 51 14.02N 35.24E
Al Qāhirah 51 30.03N 31.15E
Al Qaşr 51 25.42N 28.53E
Al Qaţrūn 50 24.55N 14.38E
Al Quşayr 51 26.04N 34.15E
Als i. 19 54.59N 9.55E
Alsace d. 12 48.25N 7.40E
Alsasua 13 42.54N 2.10W
Alston 11 54.48N 2.26W
Alta 18 70.00N 23.15E
Alta r. 18 69.50N 23.30E
Altai mts. 26 46.30N 93.30E
Altamura 15 40.50N 16.32E
Altanbulag 26 50.18N106.30E
Altea 13 38.37N 0.03W
Altenburg 16 50.59N 12.27E
Altnaharra 11 58.16N 4.26W
Alto Araguaia 47 17.19S 53.10W
Alton 9 51.08N 0.59W
Altoona 44 40.30N 78.24W
Al Ubayyiḑ 51 13.11N 30.10E
Al' Uqaylah 50 30.15N 19.12E
Al Uqşur 51 25.41N 32.24E
Alva 40 36.48N 98.40W
Alvarado 42 18.49N 95.46W
Älvdalen 19 61.14N 14.02E
Älvsbyn 18 65.39N 20.59E
Al Wajh 24 26.16N 36.28E
Alyaty 21 39.59N 49.20E
Amadeus, L. 32 24.50S130.45E
Amadjuak L. 39 65.00N 71.00W
Amagasaki 28 34.43N135.25E
Åmål 19 59.03N 12.42E
Amaliás 15 37.48N 21.21E
Amamula 53 0.17S 27.49E
Amares 13 41.38N 8.21W
Amarillo 40 35.14N101.50W
Amasya 21 40.37N 35.50E
Amazon r. see Amazonas r. 47
Amazonas r. 47 2.00S 52.00W
Ambāla 25 30.23N 76.46E
Ambarchik 23 69.39N162.27E
Amberg 16 49.27N 11.52E
Amble 8 55.20N 1.34W
Ambleside 8 54.26N 2.58W
Amboise 12 47.25N 1.00E
Ambriz 52 7.54S 13.12E
Amdo 25 32.22N 91.07E
Amersfoort 16 52.10N 5.23E
Amga 23 60.51N131.59E
Amga r. 23 62.40N135.20E
Amgu 26 45.48N137.36E
Amgun r. 23 53.10N139.47E
Amhara Plateau f. 51 10.00N 37.00E
Amiata mtn. 14 42.53N 11.37E
Amiens 12 49.54N 2.18E
Amlwch 8 53.24N 4.21W
'Ammān 24 31.57N 35.56E
Ammanford 9 51.48N 4.00W
Ammassalik 39 65.40N 38.00W
Ammókhostos 24 35.07N 33.57E
Amorgós i. 15 36.50N 25.55E
Ampala 43 13.16N 87.39W
Amrāvati 25 20.56N 77.45E
Amritsar 25 31.38N 74.53E
Amsterdam 16 52.22N 4.54E
Amu Darya r. 22 43.50N 59.00E
Amundsen G. 38 70.30N122.00W
Amur r. 23 53.17N140.00E
Anabar r. 23 72.40N113.30E
Anaconda 40 46.09N112.56W
Anadolu f. 21 38.00N 33.00E
Anadyr r. 23 65.00N176.00E
Anáfi i. 15 36.21N 25.50E
Anambas, Kepulauan is. 27 3.00N106.10E
Anápolis 47 16.19S 48.58W
Anār 24 30.54N 55.18E
Anatolia f. see Anadolu f. 21
Añatuya 48 28.26S 62.48W
Anchorage 38 61.10N150.00W
Ancón 46 11.50S 77.10W
Ancona 14 43.37N 13.33E
Andalusia 41 31.20N 86.30W
Andaman Islands 25 12.00N 92.45E
Andaman Sea 25 10.00N 95.00E
Andara 54 18.04S 21.26E
Andelot 12 48.15N 5.18E
Andenes 18 69.18N 16.10E
Anderson r. 38 69.45N129.00W
Andes mts. 49 32.40S 70.00W
Andhra Pradesh d. 25 17.00N 79.00E
Andizhan 22 40.48N 72.23E
Andorra town 12 42.30N 1.31E
Andorra 12 42.30N 1.32E
Andover 9 51.13N 1.29W
Andria 14 41.13N 16.18E
Andropov 20 58.01N 38.52E
Ándros i. 15 37.50N 24.50E
Andros I. 43 24.30N 78.00W
Andújar 13 38.02N 4.03W
Andulo 52 11.28S 16.43E
Aneto, Pico de mtn. 13 42.40N 0.19E
Angara r. 23 58.00N 93.00E
Angarsk 23 52.31N103.55E
Angaston 36 34.30S139.03E
Ånge 18 62.31N 15.40E
Ängelholm 19 56.15N 12.50E
Ångerman r. 18 63.00N 17.43E
Angers 12 47.29N 0.32W
Ångesån r. 18 66.22N 22.58E
Anglesey i. 8 53.16N 4.25W
Angoche 53 16.10S 39.57E
Angola 52 11.00S 18.00E
Angoulême 12 45.40N 0.10E
Anguilla i. 43 18.14N 63.05W
Angumu 53 0.10S 27.38E
Anholt i. 19 56.42N 11.34E
Aniak 38 61.32N159.40W
Anjouan i. 53 12.12S 44.28E
Ankara 21 39.55N 32.50E
Ānkober 51 9.32N 39.43E
Annaba 50 36.55N 7.47E
An Najaf 24 31.59N 44.19E
Annam Highlands see Annamitique, Chaîne mts. 27
Annamitique, Chaîne mts. 27 17.00N106.00E
Annan 11 54.59N 3.16W
Annan r. 11 54.58N 3.16W
Annandale f. 11 55.12N 3.25W
Anna Plains 32 19.18S121.34E
Annapurna mtn. 25 28.34N 83.50E
Ann Arbor 44 42.18N 83.43W
Annecy 12 45.54N 6.07E
Anniston 41 33.58N 85.50W
Annonay 12 45.15N 4.40E
An Nuhūd 51 12.41N 28.28E
Anoka 41 45.11N 93.20W
Anqing 26 30.40N117.03E
Ansbach 16 49.18N 10.36E
Anshan 26 41.06N122.58E
Anstruther 11 56.14N 2.42W
Antakya 21 36.12N 36.10E
Antalya 21 36.53N 39.42E
Antananarivo 3 18.55S 47.31E
Antequera 13 37.01N 4.34W
Antibes 12 43.35N 7.07E
Anticosti, Île d' i. 39 49.20N 63.00W
Antigua 42 14.33N 90.42W
Antigua i. 43 17.09N 61.49W
Antipodes Is. 30 49.42S178.50E
Antofagasta 48 23.39S 70.24W
Antrain 12 48.28N 1.30W
Antrim 10 54.43N 6.14W
Antrim d. 10 54.58N 6.20W
Antrim, Mts. of 10 55.00N 6.10W
Antwerpen 16 51.13N 4.25E
Anvik 38 62.38N160.20W
Anxi Gansu 26 40.32N 95.57E
Anyang 26 36.05N114.20E
Anzio 14 41.27N 12.37E
Aomori 26 40.50N140.43E
Aosta 14 45.43N 7.19E
Apalachee B. 41 29.30N 84.00W
Aparri 27 18.22N121.40E
Apeldoorn 16 52.13N 5.57E
Apia 30 13.48S171.45W
Apostle Is. 41 47.00N 90.30W
Apóstoles 48 27.55S 55.45W
Appalachian Mts. 41 39.30N 78.00W
Appennino mts. 14 42.00N 13.30E
Appleby 8 54.35N 2.29W
Appleton 41 44.17N 88.24W
Apucarana 45 23.34S 51.28W
Apure r. 46 7.40N 66.30W
Aquidauana 48 20.27S 55.45W
Aquila 42 18.30N103.50W
Aquitaine d. 12 44.40N 0.00
'Arab, Baḩr al r. 51 9.02N 29.28E
Arabian Sea 24 15.00N 64.00E
Aracaju 47 10.54S 37.07W
Araçatuba 45 21.12S 50.24W
Arafura Sea 27 9.00S133.00E
Aragarças 47 15.55S 52.12W
Aragón r. 13 42.20N 1.45W
Araguaia r. 47 5.20S 48.30W
Araguari r. 47 1.15N 50.05W
Arāk 24 34.06N 49.44E
Arakan Yoma mts. 25 19.30N 94.30E
Araks r. 21 40.00N 48.28E
Aral Sea see Aralskoye More sea 22
Aralsk 22 46.56N 61.43E
Aralskoye More sea 22 45.00N 60.00E
Aramac 34 22.59S145.14E
Aranda de Duero 13 41.40N 3.41W
Aran I. 10 53.07N 9.38W
Aran Is. 10 53.07N 9.38W
Aranjuez 13 40.02N 3.37W
Araouane 50 18.53N 3.31W
Araraquara 45 21.46S 48.08W
Ararat 36 37.20S143.00E
Ararat mtn. see Ağri Daği mtn. 21
Aras r. Turkey see Araks r. 21
Araxá 45 19.37S 46.50W
Arbatax 14 39.56N 9.41E
Arbroath 11 56.34N 2.35W
Arcachon 12 44.40N 1.11W
Arctic Bay town 39 73.05N 85.20W
Arctic Red r. 38 67.26N133.48W
Arctic Red River town 38 67.27N133.46W
Arda r. 15 41.39N 26.30E
Ardabīl 24 38.15N 48.18E
Ardara 10 54.46N 8.25W
Ardèche r. 12 44.31N 4.40E
Ardennes mts. 16 50.10N 5.30E
Ardila r. 13 38.10N 7.30W
Ardmore 10 51.58N 7.43W
Ardnamurchan, Pt. of 11 56.44N 6.14W
Ardrossan 11 55.38N 4.49W
Ards Pen. 10 54.30N 5.30W
Åre 18 63.25N 13.05E
Arecibo 43 18.29N 66.44W
Arena, Pt. 40 38.58N123.44W
Arendal 19 58.27N 8.48E
Arequipa 46 16.25S 71.32W
Arès 12 44.47N 1.08W
Arévalo 13 41.03N 4.43W
Arezzo 14 43.27N 11.52E
Arganda 13 40.19N 3.26W
Argelès-sur-Mer 12 42.33N 3.01E
Argens r. 12 43.10N 6.45E
Argentan 12 48.45N 0.01W
Argentina 49 36.00S 63.00W
Argentino, L. 49 50.15S 72.25W
Argenton 12 46.36N 1.30E
Argeş r. 15 44.13N 26.22E
Árgos 15 37.37N 22.45E
Argostólion 15 38.10N 20.30E
Århus 19 56.09N 10.13E
Ariano 14 41.04N 15.00E
Arica 48 18.29S 70.20W
Arima 46 10.38N 61.17W
Arinos r. 47 10.20S 57.35W
Aris 54 22.48S 17.10E
Arisaig 11 56.55N 5.51W
Ariza 13 41.19N 2.03W
Arizona d. 40 34.00N112.00W
Arkaig, Loch 11 56.58N 5.08W
Arkansas d. 41 35.00N 92.00W
Arkansas r. 41 33.50N 91.00W
Arkansas City 41 37.03N 97.02W
Arkhangel'sk 20 64.32N 41.10E
Árki i. 15 37.22N 26.45E
Arklow 10 52.47N 6.10W
Arlberg Pass 16 47.00N 10.05E
Arles 12 43.41N 4.38E
Arlington Va. 44 38.52N 77.05W
Arlon 16 49.41N 5.49E
Armadale 33 32.10S115.57E
Armagh 10 54.21N 6.41W
Armagh d. 10 54.16N 6.35W
Armavir 21 44.59N 41.10E
Armenia 46 4.32N 75.40W
Armidale 37 30.32S151.40E
Arnaud r. 39 60.00N 69.45W
Årnes 19 60.09N 11.28E
Arnhem 16 52.00N 5.55E
Arnhem, C. 34 12.10S137.00E
Arnhem B. 34 12.20S136.12E
Arnhem Land f. 34 13.10S134.30E
Arno r. 14 43.43N 10.17E
Ar Rahad 51 12.42N 30.33E
Arran i. 11 55.35N 5.14W
Arras 12 50.17N 2.46E
Arrecife 50 28.57N 13.32W
Ar Riyāḑ 24 24.39N 46.44E
Arrochar 11 56.12N 4.44W
Arrow, Lough 10 54.03N 8.20W
Ar Rub' al Khālī des. 24 19.00N 50.30E
Ar Ruşayriş 51 11.52N 34.23E
Árta 15 39.10N 20.57E
Artesia 40 32.51N104.24W
Arthur's Pass 29 42.50S171.45E
Artillery L. 38 63.09N107.52W
Artvin 21 41.12N 41.48E
Aru, Kepulauan is. 27 6.00S134.30E
Arua 53 3.02N 30.56E
Aruanã 47 14.54S 51.05W
Aruba i. 43 12.30N 70.00W
Arunachal Pradesh d. 25 28.40N 94.60E
Aruwimi r. 52 1.20N 23.36E
Arvagh 10 53.56N 7.35W
Arvidsjaur 18 65.35N 19.07E
Arzignano 14 45.31N 11.20E
Asahi dake mtn. 26 43.42N142.54E
Asansol 25 23.41N 86.59E
Aschaffenburg 16 49.58N 9.10E
Aschersleben 16 51.46N 11.28E
Ascoli Piceno 14 42.52N 13.36E
Aseb 51 13.01N 42.47E
Åseda 19 57.10N 15.20E
Ashbourne 10 53.31N 6.25W
Ashburton r. 32 21.15S115.00E
Ashburton 29 43.54S171.46E
Ashby de la Zouch 9 52.45N 1.29W
Ashcroft 38 50.43N121.17W
Asheville 41 35.35N 82.35W
Ashford Kent 9 51.08N 0.53E
Ashington 8 55.11N 1.34W
Ash Shiḩr 24 14.45N 49.36E
Ashton 54 33.49S 20.04E
Asinara i. 14 41.04N 8.18E
'Asīr f. 24 19.00N 42.00E
Askeaton 10 52.36N 9.00W
Askersund 19 58.53N 14.54E
Askim 19 59.35N 11.10E
Āsmera 51 15.20N 38.58E
Aspiring, Mt. 29 44.20S168.45E
As Saffānīyah 24 28.00N 48.48E
As Sallūm 51 31.31N 25.09E
Assam d. 25 26.30N 93.00E
Assen 16 53.00N 6.34E
Assiniboia 38 49.38N105.59W
Assis 45 22.37S 50.25W
As Suways 51 29.59N 32.33E
Asti 14 44.54N 8.13E
Astipálaia i. 15 36.35N 26.25E
Astorga 13 42.30N 6.02W
Astoria 40 46.12N123.50W
Astrakhan 21 46.22N 48.00E
Asunción 45 25.15S 57.40W
Aswān 51 24.05N 32.56E
Aswan High Dam see As Sadd al 'Ālī 51
Asyūţ 51 27.14N 31.07E
Atacama, Desierto des. 48 20.00S 69.00W
Atacama Desert see Atacama, Desierto des. 48
Atar 50 20.32N 13.08W
Atasu 22 48.42N 71.38E
'Aţbarah 51 17.42N 34.00E
'Aţbarah r. 51 17.47N 34.00E
Athabasca 38 54.44N113.15W
Athabasca r. 38 58.30N111.00W
Athabasca, L. 38 59.30N109.00W
Athenry 10 53.18N 8.45W
Athens see Athínai 15
Athens Ga. 41 33.57N 83.24W
Athínai 15 37.59N 23.42E
Athlone 10 53.26N 7.57W
Atholl, Forest of 11 56.50N 3.55W
Áthos mtn. 15 40.09N 24.19E
Atlanta Ga. 41 33.45N 84.23W
Atlantic City 44 39.22N 74.26W
Atlas Saharien mts. 50 34.20N 2.00E
Atlin 38 59.35N133.42W
Atrak r. Iran see Atrek r. 24
Ätran r. 19 56.53N 12.30E
Atrek r. 24 37.23N 54.00E
Aţ Ţā'if 24 21.15N 40.21E
Aubagne 12 43.17N 5.35E
Aube r. 12 48.30N 3.37E
Aubin 12 44.32N 2.14E
Aubusson 12 45.57N 2.11E
Auch 12 43.40N 0.36E
Auchterarder 11 56.18N 3.43W
Auckland 29 36.55S174.45E
Auckland Is. 30 50.35S166.00E
Aude r. 12 43.13N 2.20E
Augrabies Falls f. 54 28.33S 20.27E
Augsburg 16 48.21N 10.54E
Augusta Ga. 41 33.29N 82.00W
Aulnay 12 46.02N 0.22W
Aulne r. 12 48.30N 4.11W
Aumale 12 49.46N 1.45E
Aurich 16 53.28N 7.29E
Aurillac 12 44.56N 2.26E
Aus 54 26.41S 16.14E
Austin Minn. 41 43.40N 92.58W

56

Fannich, Loch 11 57.38N 5.00W
Faradje 53 3.45N 29.43E
Fareham 9 50.52N 1.11W
Farewell, C. 29 40.30S172.35E
Fargo 41 46.52N 96.59W
Farnborough 9 51.17N 0.46W
Farne Is. 8 55.38N 1.36W
Farnham 9 51.13N 0.49W
Faro 13 37.01N 7.56W
Faroe Is. 18 62.00N 7.00W
Fårösund 19 57.52N 19.03E
Farrell 44 41.13N 80.31W
Farsund 19 58.05N 6.48E
Farvel, Kap c. 39 60.00N 44.20W
Fâurei 17 45.04N 27.15E
Fauske 18 67.17N 15.25E
Favignana i. 14 37.57N 12.19E
Faxe r. 18 63.15N 17.15E
Fayetteville N.C. 41 35.03N 78.53W
Fdérik 50 22.30N 12.30W
Feale r. 10 52.28N 9.37W
Fécamp 12 49.45N 0.23E
Feeagh, Lough 10 53.56N 9.35W
Fehmarn i. 16 54.30N 11.05E
Feira 53 15.30S 30.27E
Feldkirch 16 47.15N 9.38E
Felixstowe 9 51.58N 1.20E
Feodosiya 21 45.03N 35.23E
Fergana 22 40.23N 71.19E
Fergus Falls town 41 46.18N 96.00W
Fermanagh d. 10 54.21N 7.40W
Fermoy 10 52.08N 8.17W
Ferrara 14 44.49N 11.38E
Ferret, Cap c. 12 44.42N 1.16W
Fès 50 34.05N 5.00W
Feshi 52 6.08S 18.12E
Fetlar i. 11 60.37N 0.52W
Fife d. 11 56.10N 3.10W
Fife Ness c. 11 56.17N 2.36W
Figeac 12 44.32N 2.01E
Figueira da Foz 13 40.09N 8.51W
Figueres 13 42.16N 2.57E
Fiji 30 18.00S178.00E
Filey 8 54.13N 0.18W
Findhorn r. 11 57.38N 3.37W
Findlay 44 41.02N 83.40W
Finisterre, Cabo de c. 13 42.54N 9.16W
Finland 20 64.30N 27.00E
Finland, G. of 19 59.30N 24.00E
Finlay r. 38 56.30N124.40W
Finn r. 10 54.50N 7.30W
Firenze 14 43.46N 11.15E
Firth of Clyde est. 11 55.35N 4.53W
Firth of Forth est. 11 56.05N 3.00W
Firth of Lorn est. 11 56.20N 5.40W
Firth of Tay est. 11 56.24N 3.08W
Fishguard 9 51.59N 4.59W
Fitzroy Crossing 32 18.13S125.33E
Fizi 53 4.18S 28.56E
Flagstaff 40 35.12N111.38W
Flåm 19 60.50N 7.07E
Flamborough Head 8 54.06N 0.05W
Flannan Is. 11 58.16N 7.40W
Flathead L. 40 47.50N114.05W
Fleetwood 8 53.55N 3.01W
Flen 19 59.04N 16.35E
Flensburg 16 54.47N 9.27E
Flinders r. 34 17.30S140.45E
Flinders I. Tas. 35 40.00S148.00E
Flinders Range mts. 36 31.25S138.45E
Flin Flon 39 54.47N101.51W
Flint U.K. 8 53.15N 3.07W
Flint U.S.A. 44 43.03N 83.40W
Flint r. Ga. 41 30.52N 84.35W
Flinton 35 27.54S149.34E
Florence see Firenze 14
Florence, L. 36 28.52S138.08E
Flores i. 27 8.40S121.20E
Flores, Laut sea 27 7.00S121.00E
Flores Sea see Flores, Laut sea 27
Florianópolis 45 27.35S 48.34W
Florida d. 41 29.00N 82.00W
Flórina 15 40.48N 21.25E
Florö 19 61.36N 5.00E
Flushing see Vlissingen 16
Focșani 17 45.40N 27.12E
Foggia 14 41.28N 15.33E
Foix 12 42.57N 1.35E
Folgares 52 14.55S 15.03E
Folkestone 9 51.05N 1.11E
Fond du Lac 38 59.20N107.09W
Fontainebleau 12 48.24N 2.42E
Fontenay 12 46.28N 0.48W
Forbes 37 33.24S148.03E
Foreland Pt. 9 51.15N 3.47W
Forest of Bowland hills 8 53.57N 2.30W
Forest of Dean f. 9 51.48N 2.32W
Forfar 11 56.38N 2.54W
Formby Pt. 8 53.34N 3.07W
Formentera i. 13 38.41N 1.30E
Formosa see Taiwan 26
Forres 11 57.37N 3.38W
Forrest 33 30.49S128.03E
Fort Albany 39 52.15N 81.35W
Fortaleza 47 3.45S 38.35W
Fort Augustus 11 57.09N 4.41W
Fort Beaufort 54 32.46S 26.36E
Fort Chimo 39 58.10N 68.15W
Fort Chipewyan 38 58.46N111.09W
Fort Collins 40 40.35N105.05W
Fort-de-France 43 14.36N 61.05W
Fort Frances 39 48.37N 93.23W
Fort George 39 53.50N 79.01W
Fort Good Hope 38 66.16N128.37W
Forth r. 11 56.06N 3.48W
Fort Lauderdale 41 26.08N 80.08W
Fort Maguire 53 13.38S 34.59E
Fort McMurray 38 56.45N111.27W
Fort McPherson 38 67.29N134.50W
Fort Myers 41 26.39N 81.51W
Fort Nelson 38 58.48N122.44W
Fort Norman 38 64.55N125.29W
Fort Portal 53 0.40N 30.17E
Fort Randall 38 55.10N162.47W
Fort Reliance 38 62.45N109.08W
Fort Resolution 38 61.10N113.39W
Fortrose 11 57.34N 4.09W
Fort St. John 38 56.14N120.55W
Fort Scott 41 37.52N 94.43W
Fort Severn 39 56.00N 87.40W
Fort Simpson 38 61.46N121.15W
Fort Smith d. 38 63.30N118.00W
Fort Smith U.S.A. 41 35.22N 94.27W
Fort Vermilion 38 58.22N115.59W
Fort Wayne 44 41.05N 85.08W
Fort William 11 56.49N 5.07W
Fort Worth 41 32.45N 97.20W
Fort Yukon 38 66.35N145.20W
Fougères 12 48.21N 1.12W
Foula i. 11 60.08N 2.05W
Foulness I. 9 51.35N 0.55E
Foulwind, C. 29 41.45S171.30E
Foveaux Str. 29 46.40S168.00E
Fowey 9 50.20N 4.39W
Foxe Channel 39 65.00N 80.00W
Foxton 29 40.27S175.18E
Foyle r. 10 55.00N 7.20W
Foyle, Lough 10 55.05N 7.10W
Foz do Iguaçu 45 25.33S 54.31W
Franca 45 20.33S 47.27W
France 12 47.00N 2.00E
Franceville 52 1.38S 13.31E
Francistown 54 21.12S 27.29E
Frankfort 54 27.15S 28.30E
Frankfurt E. Germany 16 52.20N 14.32E
Frankfurt W. Germany 16 50.06N 8.41E
Franz Josef Land is. see Frantsa Iosifa, Zemlya ya 22
Fraser r. B.C. 38 49.05N123.00W
Fraserburg 54 31.55S 21.29E
Fraserburgh 11 57.42N 2.00W
Fredericia 19 55.35N 9.46E
Fredericksburg Va. 41 38.18N 77.30W
Fredericton 44 45.57N 66.40W
Frederikshåb 39 62.05N 49.30W
Frederikshavn 19 57.26N 10.32E
Fredrikstad 19 59.13N 10.57E
Freeport 43 26.40N 78.30W
Freetown 50 8.30N 13.17W
Freiburg 16 48.00N 7.52E
Fréjus 12 43.26N 6.44E
Fremantle 33 32.07S115.44E
Freshford 10 52.44N 7.23W
Fresno 40 36.41N119.57W
Fribourg 16 46.50N 7.10E
Friedrichshafen 16 47.39N 9.29E
Frobisher Bay town 39 63.45N 68.30W
Frohavet est. 18 63.55N 9.05E
Frome 9 51.16N 2.17W
Frome, L. 36 30.48S139.48E
Fröya i. 18 63.45N 8.45E
Frunze 22 42.53N 74.46E
Fuerte r. 42 25.42N109.20W
Fuji san mtn. 28 35.22N138.44E
Fukui 26 36.04N136.12E
Fukuoka 26 33.39N130.21E
Fulda 16 50.35N 9.45E
Funabashi 28 35.42N139.59E
Funchal 50 32.38N 16.54W
Fundy, B. of 44 45.00N 66.00W
Furancungo 53 14.51S 33.38E
Furneaux Group is. 35 40.15S148.15E
Fürstenwalde 16 52.22N 14.04E
Fürth 16 49.28N 11.00E
Fushun 26 41.50N123.55E
Fuyu 26 45.12N124.49E
Fuzhou 26 26.09N119.21E
Fyne, Loch 11 55.55N 5.23W

G

Gabela 52 10.52S 14.24E
Gabès 50 33.52N 10.06E
Gabon 52 0.00 12.00E
Gabon r. 52 0.15N 10.00E
Gaborone 54 24.45S 25.55E
Gadsden 41 34.00N 86.00W
Gaeta 14 41.13N 13.35E
Gagnoa 50 6.04N 5.55W
Gagnon 39 51.55N 68.10W
Gaillac 12 43.54N 1.53E
Gainesville Fla. 41 29.37N 82.31W
Gainsborough 8 53.23N 0.46W
Gairdner, L. 36 31.30S136.00E
Gairloch 11 57.43N 5.40W
Galana r. 53 3.12S 40.09E
Galapagos, Islas is. 31 0.30S 90.30W
Galashiels 11 55.37N 2.49W
Galaţi 17 45.27N 27.59E
Galena Alas. 38 64.43N157.00W
Galesburg 41 40.58N 90.22W
Galle 25 6.01N 80.13E
Gállego r. 13 41.40N 0.55W
Gallipoli 15 40.02N 18.01E
Galloway f. 11 55.00N 4.28W
Gallup 40 35.32N108.46W
Galston 11 55.36N 4.23W
Galty Mts. 10 52.20N 8.10W
Galveston 41 29.17N 94.48W
Galvez 48 32.03S 61.14W
Galway 10 53.17N 9.04W
Galway d. 10 53.25N 9.00W
Gambia 50 13.30N 15.00W
Gambia r. 50 13.28N 15.55W
Gamboma 52 1.50S 15.58E
Ganda 52 12.58S 14.39E
Gandajika 52 6.46S 23.58E
Gander 39 48.58N 54.34W
Gandía 13 38.59N 0.11W
Ganga r. 25 23.22N 90.32E
Ganges r. see Ganga r. 25
Ganzhou 26 25.49N114.50E
Gao 50 16.19N 0.09W
Gap 12 44.33N 6.05E
Gara, Lough 10 53.57N 8.27W
Gard r. 12 43.52N 4.40E
Garda, Lago di l. 14 45.40N 10.40E
Garies 54 30.34S 18.00E
Garissa 53 0.27S 39.49E
Garmisch Partenkirchen 16 47.30N 11.05E
Garonne r. 12 45.00N 0.37W
Garoua 50 9.17N 13.22E
Garron Pt. 10 55.03N 5.57W
Garry L. 39 66.00N100.00W
Garut 27 7.15S107.55E
Garvão 13 37.42N 8.21W
Garve 11 57.37N 4.41W
Garvie Mts. 29 45.15S169.00E
Gary 44 41.34N 87.20W
Gascogne, Golfe de g. 12 44.00N 2.40W
Gascony, G. of see Gascogne, Golfe de 12
Gascoyne r. 32 25.00S113.40E
Gaspé 39 48.50N 64.30W
Gaspé, Péninsule de pen. 44 48.30N 65.00W
Gata, Sierra de mts. 13 40.20N 6.30W
Gatehouse of Fleet 11 54.53N 4.12W
Gateshead 8 54.57N 1.35W
Gatineau r. 44 45.27N 75.40W
Gavá 13 41.18N 2.00E
Gävle 19 60.40N 17.10E
Gavrion 15 37.52N 24.46E
Gawler 36 34.38S138.44E
Gcuwa 54 32.20S 28.09E
Gdańsk 17 54.22N 18.38E
Gdov 20 58.48N 27.52E
Gdynia 17 54.31N 18.30E
Geel 16 51.10N 5.00E
Geelong 36 38.10S144.26E
Geidam 50 12.55N 11.55E
Gelsenkirchen 16 51.30N 7.05E
Gemena 52 3.14N 19.48E
Gemlik 21 40.26N 29.10E
General Pico 49 35.38S 63.46W
Geneva see Genève 16
Geneva, L. see Léman, Lac l. 16
Genève 16 46.13N 6.09E
Genoa see Genova 14
Genoa, G. of see Genova, Golfo di g. 14
Genova 14 44.24N 8.54E
Gent 16 51.02N 3.42E
George 54 33.57S 22.27E
George, L. N.S.W. 37 35.07S149.22E
George Town Tas. 35 41.04S146.48E
Georgetown Cayman Is. 43 19.20N 81.23W
Georgetown Guyana 46 6.46N 58.10W
George Town Malaysia 27 5.30N100.16E
Georgia d. 41 33.00N 83.00W
Gera 16 50.51N 12.11E
Geraldine 29 44.05S171.15E
Geraldton 33 28.49S114.36E
Germiston 54 26.14S 28.10E
Geyve 21 40.32N 30.18E
Ghana 50 8.00N 1.00W
Ghanzi 54 21.42S 21.39E
Ghardaïa 50 32.20N 3.40E
Ghāt 50 24.59N 10.11E
Gibraltar 13 36.07N 5.22W
Gibraltar, Str. of 13 36.00N 5.25W
Gibson Desert 32 24.30S123.00E
Giessen 16 50.35N 8.42E
Gifu 28 35.25N136.45E
Gigha i. 11 55.41N 5.44W
Gijón 13 43.32N 5.40W
Gila r. 40 32.45N114.30W
Gilé 53 16.10S 38.17E
Gilgandra 37 31.42S148.40E
Gilgit 25 35.54N 74.20E
Gill, Lough 10 54.15N 8.14W
Gillingham Kent 9 51.24N 0.33E
Girdle Ness 11 57.06N 2.02W
Giresun 21 40.55N 38.25E
Girona 13 41.59N 2.49E
Gironde r. 12 45.35N 1.00W
Girvan 11 55.15N 4.51W
Gisborne 29 38.41S178.02E
Gizhiga 23 62.00N160.34E
Gladstone Qld. 34 23.52S151.16E
Glåma r. 19 59.15N 10.55E
Glasgow 11 55.52N 4.15W
Glastonbury 9 51.09N 2.42W
Glazov 20 58.09N 52.42E
Glen Affric f. 11 57.15N 5.03W
Glen Coe f. 11 56.40N 5.03W
Glendale Calif. 40 34.09N118.20W
Glendive 40 47.08N104.42W
Glengarriff 10 51.45N 9.33W
Glen Garry f. Highland 11 57.03N 5.04W
Glen Head 10 54.44N 8.46W
Glen Innes 37 29.42S151.45E
Glen Mór f. 11 57.15N 4.30W
Glenrothes 11 56.12N 3.10W
Glenshee f. 11 56.45N 3.25W
Głogów 16 51.40N 16.06E
Gloucester 9 51.52N 2.15W
Gloucestershire d. 9 51.45N 2.00W
Goa d. 25 15.30N 74.00E
Goat Fell mtn. 11 55.37N 5.12W
Gobi des. 26 45.00N108.00E
Godalming 9 51.11N 0.37W
Godāvari r. 25 16.40N 82.15E
Godhavn 39 69.20N 53.30W
Godthåb 39 64.10N 51.40W
Göksun 21 38.03N 36.30E
Golden B. 29 40.45S172.50E
Golden Vale f. 10 52.30N 8.07W
Golspie 11 57.58N 3.58W
Goma 53 1.37S 29.10E
Gombe r. 53 4.43S 31.30E
Gongga Shan mtn. 26 29.30N101.30E
Good Hope, C. of 54 34.21S 18.28E
Goole 8 53.42N 0.52W
Goose L. 40 41.55N120.25W
Göppingen 16 48.43N 9.39E
Gorakhpur 25 26.45N 83.22E
Gore 29 46.06S168.58E
Gori 21 41.59N 44.05E
Gorki see Gor'kiy 20
Gor'kiy 20 56.20N 44.00E
Gorzów Wielkopolski 16 52.42N 15.12E
Gosford 37 33.25S151.18E
Goslar 16 51.54N 10.25E
Gospić 16 44.34N 15.23E
Gosport 9 50.48N 1.08W
Göteborg 19 57.43N 11.58E
Gotha 16 50.57N 10.43E
Gothenburg see Göteborg 19
Gotland i. 19 57.30N 18.33E
Göttingen 16 51.32N 9.57E
Goulburn r. 37 36.08S144.30E
Gourdon 12 44.45N 1.22E
Gouré 50 13.59N 10.15E
Gournay 12 49.29N 1.44E
Gourock Range mts. 37 35.45S149.25E
Gower pen. 9 51.37N 4.10W
Goya 48 29.10S 59.20W
Goyder r. 34 12.38S135.11E
Gozo i. 14 36.03N 14.16E
Grahamstown 54 33.18S 26.30E
Grampian d. 11 57.22N 2.35W
Grampian Mts. 11 56.55N 4.00W
Granada 13 37.10N 3.35W
Granby 44 45.23N 72.44W
Gran Canaria i. 50 28.00N 15.30W
Gran Chaco f. 48 22.00S 60.00W
Grand r. S.Dak. 40 45.40N100.32W
Grand Bahama I. 43 26.35N 78.00W
Grand Canyon f. 40 36.15N113.00W
Grand Cayman i. 43 19.20N 81.30W
Grande r. 48 15.10S 64.55W
Grande r. Minas Gerais 48 20.00S 51.00W
Grande Comore i. 53 11.35S 43.20E
Grande Prairie town 38 55.10N118.52W
Grand Forks 41 47.57N 97.05W
Grand Island town 40 40.56N 98.21W
Grand Junction 40 39.04N108.33W
Grand Manan I. 44 44.38N 66.50W
Grand Rapids town Mich. 44 42.57N 85.40W
Grand St. Bernard, Col du pass 16 45.52N 7.11E
Grand Teton mtn. 40 43.45N110.50W
Grangemouth 11 56.01N 3.44W
Grantham 8 52.55N 0.39W
Grantown-on-Spey 11 57.20N 3.38W
Grants Pass town 40 42.26N123.20W
Granville 12 48.50N 1.35W
Graskop 54 24.55S 30.50E
Grasse 12 43.40N 6.56E
Gravesend 9 51.27N 0.24E
Gray 12 47.27N 5.35E
Grays 9 51.29N 0.20E
Graz 16 47.05N 15.22E
Great Artesian Basin f. 34 26.30S143.02E
Great Australian Bight 33 33.10S129.30E
Great Barrier I. 29 36.15S175.30E
Great Barrier Reef f. 34 16.30S146.30E
Great Basin f. 40 39.00N115.30W
Great Bear L. 38 66.00N120.00W
Great Blasket I. 10 52.05N 10.32W
Great Dividing Range mts. 37 29.00S152.00E
Great Driffield 8 54.01N 0.26W
Greater London d. 9 51.31N 0.06W
Greater Manchester d. 8 53.30N 2.18W
Great Falls town 40 47.30N111.16W
Great Karoo f. 54 32.40S 22.20E
Great Kei r. 54 32.39S 28.23E
Great L. 35 41.50S146.43E
Great Malvern 9 52.07N 2.19W
Great Namaland f. 54 25.30S 17.20E
Great Ouse r. 8 52.47N 0.23E
Great Salt L. 40 41.10N112.40W
Great Sandy Desert 32 20.30S123.35E
Great Slave L. 38 61.30N114.20W
Great Victoria Desert 33 29.00S127.30E
Great Whernside mtn. 8 54.09N 1.59W
Great Yarmouth 9 52.40N 1.45E
Greece 15 39.00N 22.00E
Greeley 40 40.26N104.43W
Green r. 40 38.20N109.53W
Greenhills 33 31.58S117.01E
Greenland 39 68.00N 45.00W
Greenlaw 11 55.43N 2.28W
Greenock 11 55.57N 4.45W
Greensboro N.C. 41 36.03N 79.50W
Greenville S.C. 41 34.52N 82.25W
Grenå 19 56.25N 10.53E
Grenada 46 12.07N 61.40W
Grenada i. 43 12.15N 61.45W
Grenoble 12 45.11N 5.43E
Gretna 11 55.00N 3.04W
Grey r. 29 42.28S171.13E
Greymouth 29 42.28S171.12E
Grey Range mts. 35 27.00S143.35E
Greystones 10 53.09N 6.04W
Grim, C. 35 40.45S144.45E
Grimsby 8 53.35N 0.05W
Grodno 17 53.40N 23.50E
Groningen 16 53.13N 6.35E
Groot r. C.P. r. 54 33.58S 25.03E
Groote Eylandt i. 34 14.00S136.40E
Grootfontein 54 19.32S 18.07E
Grossenbrode 16 54.23N 11.07E
Gross Glockner mtn. 16 47.05N 12.50E
Groundhog r. 44 49.43N 81.58W
Groznyy 21 43.21N 45.42E
Guadalajara 42 20.30N103.20W
Guadalcanal i. 30 9.32S160.12E
Guadalete r. 13 36.37N 6.15W
Guadalmena r. 13 38.00N 3.50W
Guadalquivir r. 13 36.50N 6.20W
Guadalupe 42 25.41N100.15W
Guadalupe, Isla de i. 40 29.00N118.25W
Guadarrama r. 13 39.55N 4.10W
Guadarrama, Sierra de mts. 13 41.00N 3.50W
Guadeloupe i. 43 16.20N 61.40W
Guadiana r. 13 37.10N 7.36W
Guadix 13 37.19N 3.08W
Guaira 48 24.04S 54.15W
Gualeguay 49 33.10S 59.20W
Gualeguaychu 49 33.00S 58.30W
Guam i. 30 13.30N 144.40E
Guangxi Zhuangzu d. 26 23.30N109.00E
Guangzhou 26 23.08N113.20E
Guaporé r. 48 12.00S 65.15W
Guarapuava 45 25.22S 51.28W
Guarda 13 40.32N 7.17W
Guardo 13 42.47N 4.50W
Guatemala 43 15.40N 90.00W
Guatemala town 42 14.38N 90.22W
Guaviare r. 46 4.00N 67.35W
Guayaquil 46 2.13S 79.54W
Guaymas 42 27.59N110.54W
Gubin 16 51.59N 14.42E
Guecho 13 43.21N 3.01W
Guéret 12 46.10N 1.52E
Guernsey i. 9 49.27N 2.35W
Guiana 47 3.40N 53.00W
Guiana Highlands 46 4.00N 59.00W
Guildford 9 51.14N 0.35W
Guilin 26 25.20N110.10E
Guinea 50 10.30N 10.30W
Guinea, G. of 50 2.00N 1.00W
Guinea Bissau 50 12.00N 15.30W
Güines 43 22.50N 82.02W
Guingamp 12 48.34N 3.09W
Güiria 46 10.37N 62.21W
Guiyang 26 26.31N106.39E
Gujarat d. 25 22.20N 70.30E
Gulu 53 2.46N 32.21E
Gundagai 37 35.07S148.05E
Gungu 52 5.43S 19.20E
Gunnedah 37 30.59S150.15E
Gürün 21 38.44N 37.15E
Guruve 53 16.42S 30.40E
Guyana 46 4.40N 59.00W
Gwādar 24 25.07N 62.19E
Gwai r. 54 17.59S 26.55E
Gwalior 25 26.12N 78.10E
Gwanda 54 20.59S 29.00E
Gweebarra B. 10 54.52N 8.28W
Gwent d. 9 51.44N 3.00W
Gweru 54 19.25S 29.50E
Gwynedd d. 8 53.00N 4.00W
Györ 17 47.41N 17.40E

H

Haarlem 16 52.22N 4.38E
Haddington 11 55.57N 2.47W
Ḥadramawt f. 24 16.30N 49.30E
Hagerstown 44 39.39N 77.43W
Ha Giang 26 22.50N105.00E
Hague, Cap de la c. 12 49.44N 1.56W
Haikou 26 20.03N110.27E
Ḥā'il 24 27.31N 41.45E
Hailsham 9 50.52N 0.17E
Hainan i. 27 19.00N109.30E
Haines Alas. 38 59.11N135.23W
Hai Phòng 26 20.48N106.40E
Haiti 43 19.00N 73.00W
Hakkâri 21 37.36N 43.45E
Hakodate 26 41.46N140.44E
Ḥalab 24 36.14N 37.10E
Halberstadt 16 51.54N 11.04E
Halden 19 59.09N 11.23E
Haliburton Highlands 44 45.03N 78.03W
Halifax Canada 39 44.38N 63.35W
Halifax U.K. 8 53.43N 1.51W
Halifax B. 34 18.50S146.30E
Halle 16 51.28N 11.58E
Hall's Creek town 32 18.17S127.44E
Hallstavik 19 60.03N 18.36E
Halmahera i. 27 0.45N128.00E
Halmstad 19 56.39N 12.50E
Hälsingborg 19 56.03N 12.42E
Haltwhistle 8 54.58N 2.27W
Hamamatsu 28 34.42N137.44E
Hamar 19 60.48N 11.06E
Hamburg 16 53.33N 10.00E
Hameln 16 52.06N 9.21E
Hamersley Range mts. 32 22.00S118.00E
Hami 26 42.40N 93.30E
Hamilton r. 35 27.12S135.28E
Hamilton Canada 44 43.15N 79.51W
Hamilton New Zealand 29 37.46S175.18E
Hamilton U.K. 11 55.46N 4.10W
Hamilton Ohio 44 39.23N 84.33W
Hammerfest 18 70.40N 23.42E
Hampshire d. 9 51.03N 1.20W
Handa 28 34.53N136.56E
Handeni 53 5.25S 38.04E
Hangzhou 26 30.14N120.08E
Hannibal Mo. 41 39.41N 91.25W
Hannover 16 52.23N 9.44E
Hà Nôi 26 21.01N105.53E
Hanoi see Hà Nôi 26
Hanover 54 31.04S 24.25E
Haparanda 18 65.50N 24.10E
Ḥaraḍ 24 24.12N 49.08E
Harare 54 17.49S 31.04E
Harbin 26 45.45N126.41E
Hardangerfjorden est. 19 60.10N 6.00E
Harding 54 30.34S 29.52E
Hargeysa 51 9.31N 44.02E
Har Hu l. 26 38.20N 97.40E
Hari r. 27 1.00S104.15E
Harlech 8 52.52N 4.08W
Harlow 9 51.47N 0.08E
Harris i. 11 57.50N 6.55W
Harris, Sd. of 11 57.43N 7.05W
Harrisburg Penn. 44 40.16N 76.52W
Harrogate 8 53.59N 1.32W
Harrow 9 51.35N 0.21W
Harstad 18 68.48N 16.30E
Hartford 44 41.45N 72.42W
Hartland Pt. 9 51.01N 4.32W
Hartlepool 8 54.42N 1.11W
Harwich 9 51.56N 1.18E
Haryana d. 25 29.15N 76.30E
Haslemere 9 51.05N 0.41W
Hässleholm 19 56.09N 13.46E
Hastings New Zealand 29 39.39S176.52E
Hastings U.K. 9 50.51N 0.36E
Hatfield 9 51.46N 0.13W
Hattiesburg 41 31.25N 89.19W
Hauge 19 58.18N 6.15E
Haugesund 19 59.25N 5.18E
Hauraki G. 29 36.30S175.00E
Havana see La Habana 43
Havant 9 50.51N 0.59W
Haverfordwest 9 51.48N 4.59W
Haverhill 9 52.06N 0.27E
Havre 40 48.34N109.45W
Hawaii d. 40 21.00N156.00W
Hawaii i. Hawaii 40 19.30N155.30W
Hawaiian Is. 40 21.00N157.00W
Hawea, L. 29 44.30S169.15E
Hawera 29 39.35S174.19E
Hawick 11 55.25N 2.47W
Hawke, C. 37 32.12S152.33E
Hawke B. 29 39.18S177.15E
Hawthorne 40 38.13N118.37W
Hay 37 34.31S144.31E
Hayes r. 39 57.00N 92.30W
Hay-on-Wye 9 52.04N 3.09W
Hazelton 38 55.16N127.18W
Hazleton 44 40.58N 75.59W
Heanor 8 53.01N 1.20W
Hebel 37 28.55S147.49E
Hebron 39 58.05N 62.30W
Heerenveen 16 52.57N 5.55E
Hefei 26 31.50N117.16E
Heidelberg 16 49.25N 8.42E
Heilbron 54 27.16S 27.57E
Heilbronn 16 49.08N 9.14E
Hekou 26 22.39N103.57E
Helena 40 46.35N112.00W
Helensburgh 11 56.01N 4.44W
Helmsdale r. 11 58.05N 3.39W
Helsingfors see Helsinki 19
Helsingör 19 56.02N 12.37E
Helsinki 19 60.08N 25.00E
Helston 9 50.07N 5.17W
Hemel Hempstead 9 51.46N 0.28W
Hemsedal 19 60.52N 8.34E
Henares r. 13 40.26N 3.35W
Hendaye 12 43.22N 1.46W
Hengelo 7 52.16N 6.46E
Hengyang 26 26.52N112.35E
Herāt 24 34.20N 62.12E
Hereford 9 52.04N 2.43W
Hereford and Worcester d. 9 52.08N 2.30W
Herford 16 52.07N 8.40E
Hermidale 37 31.33S146.44E
Herne Bay town 9 51.23N 1.10E
Herning 19 56.08N 8.59E
Hertford 9 51.48N 0.05W
Hertfordshire d. 9 51.51N 0.05W
Hexham 8 54.58N 2.06W
Heysham 8 54.03N 2.53W
Heywood 8 53.36N 2.13W
Highland d. 11 57.42N 5.00W
High Peak mtn. 8 53.22N 1.48W
High Wycombe 9 51.38N 0.46W
Hikurangi mtn. 29 37.50S178.10E
Hildesheim 16 52.09N 9.58E
Hillston 37 33.30S145.33E
Hilo Hawaii 40 19.42N155.04W
Hilversum 16 52.14N 5.12E
Himachal Pradesh d. 25 32.05N 77.15E
Himalaya mts. 25 29.00N 84.30E
Ḥimş 24 34.44N 36.43E
Hinckley 9 52.33N 1.21W
Hindmarsh, L. 36 36.03S141.53E
Hindu Kush mts. 25 36.40N 70.00E
Hiroshima 26 34.23N132.27E
Hirson 12 49.56N 4.05E
Hispaniola i. 43 19.00N 71.00W
Hitchin 9 51.57N 0.16W
Hjälmaren l. 19 59.15N 15.45E
Hjörring 19 57.28N 9.59E
Hobart 35 42.54S147.18E
Ho Chi Minh City see Thành Pho Ho Chí Min 27
Hof 16 50.19N 11.56E
Höfn 18 64.16N 15.10W
Hofors 19 60.33N 16.17E
Hohhot 26 40.49N111.37E
Hokitika 29 42.42S170.59E
Hokkaidō i. 26 43.30N143.00E
Holland Mich. 44 42.46N 86.06W
Holstebro 19 56.21N 8.38E
Holt 8 52.55N 1.04E
Holyhead 8 53.18N 4.38W
Holy I. England 8 55.41N 1.47W
Holy I. Wales 8 53.15N 4.38W
Holywood 10 54.38N 5.50W
Homer Alas. 38 59.40N151.37W
Homer Tunnel 29 44.40S168.15E
Homoine 54 23.45S 35.09E
Honduras 43 14.30N 87.00W
Honfleur 12 49.25N 0.14E
Hong Kong 26 22.15N114.15E
Hongshui He r. 26 23.20N110.04E
Honiton 9 50.48N 3.13W
Honolulu Hawaii 40 21.19N157.50W
Honshū i. 26 36.00N138.00E
Hoopstad 54 27.48S 25.52E
Hoorn 16 52.38N 5.03E
Hoover Dam 40 36.01N114.45W
Hopetoun Vic. 36 35.43S142.20E
Hopetown 54 29.37S 24.04E
Horn, C. see Hornos, Cabo de c. 49
Horncastle 8 53.13N 0.08W
Hornos, Cabo de c. 49 55.47S 67.00W
Hornsea 8 53.55N 0.10W
Horsens 19 55.52N 9.52E
Horsham 9 51.04N 0.20W
Hospitalet de Llobregat 13 41.20N 2.06E
Hotan 25 37.07N 79.57E
Hotazel 54 27.16S 22.57E
Hoting 18 64.07N 16.10E
Houndé 50 11.34N 3.31W
Houston Tex. 41 29.45N 95.25W
Hovd 26 46.40N 90.45E
Hove 9 50.50N 0.10W
Howe, C. 37 37.30S149.59E
Howitt, Mt. 37 37.15S146.40E
Howrah 25 22.35N 88.20E
Hoy i. 11 58.51N 3.17W
Huabei Pingyuan f. 26 36.32N108.14E
Huambo 52 12.47S 15.44E
Huancayo 46 12.05S 75.12W
Huang He r. 26 38.00N118.40E
Huánuco 46 9.55S 76.11W
Hubli 25 15.20N 75.14E
Hucknall 8 53.03N 1.12W
Huddersfield 8 53.38N 1.49W
Hudiksvall 19 61.44N 17.07E
Hudson r. 44 40.42N 74.02W
Hudson B. 39 58.00N 86.00W
Hudson Str. 39 62.00N 70.00W
Hue 27 16.28N107.42E
Huelva 13 37.15N 6.56W
Huelva r. 13 37.25N 6.00W
Huesca 13 42.02N 0.25W
Hughenden 34 20.51S144.12E
Huiarau Range mts. 29 38.20S177.15E
Huixtla 42 15.09N 92.30W
Hull 44 45.26N 75.45W
Hultsfred 19 57.29N 15.50E
Humansdorp 54 34.02S 24.45E
Humber r. 8 53.40N 0.12W
Humberside d. 8 53.48N 0.35W
Humboldt r. 40 40.02N118.31W
Hün 50 29.06N 15.57E
Hungary 17 47.30N 19.00E
Hüngnam 26 39.49N127.40E
Hunsrück mts. 16 49.44N 7.05E
Hunstanton 8 52.57N 0.30E
Huntingdon 9 52.20N 0.11W
Huntsville Ala. 41 34.44N 86.35W
Huron, L. 44 44.30N 82.15W
Huskvarna 19 57.48N 14.16E
Husum 16 54.29N 9.04E
Hwange 54 18.20S 26.29E
Hyde 8 53.26N 2.06W
Hyderābād India 25 17.22N 78.26E
Hyderābād Pakistan 25 25.22N 68.22E
Hyères 12 43.07N 6.08E
Hyndman Peak 40 43.46N113.55W
Hythe Kent 9 51.04N 1.05E

I

Ibadan 50 7.23N 3.56E
Ibagué 46 4.25N 75.20W
Ibarra 46 0.23N 78.05W
Ibi 50 8.11N 9.44E
Ibicaraí 47 14.52S 39.37W
Ibina r. 53 1.00N 28.40E
Ibiza i. 13 39.00N 1.23E
Ibotirama 47 12.13S 43.12W
Iceland 18 64.45N 18.00W
Ichinomiya 28 35.18N136.48E
Idah 50 7.05N 6.45E
Idaho d. 40 45.00N115.00W
Ídhra i. 15 37.20N 23.32E
Ierápetra 15 35.00N 25.45E
Iesi 14 43.32N 13.15E
Iesolo 14 45.32N 12.38E
Igoumenítsa 15 39.32N 20.14E
Iguaçu r. 45 25.33S 54.35W
Iguala 42 18.21N 99.31W
Iisalmi 18 63.34N 27.11E
IJsselmeer l. 16 52.45N 5.20E
Ijuí 45 28.23S 53.55W
Ikaría i. 15 37.35N 26.10E
Ikelemba r. 52 0.08N 18.19E
Ilebo 52 4.20S 20.35E
Ilesha Oyo 50 7.38N 4.45E
Ilfracombe 9 51.13N 4.08W
Iligan 27 8.12N124.13E
Ilkley 8 53.56N 1.49W
Illinois d. 41 40.00N 89.00W
Ilminster 9 50.55N 2.56W
Ilorin 50 8.32N 4.34E
Imala 53 14.39S 39.34E
Immingham 8 53.37N 0.12W
Imphāl 25 24.47N 93.55E
Inca 13 39.43N 2.54E
Inch'on 26 37.30N126.38E
India 25 23.00N 78.00E
Indiana d. 44 40.00N 86.15W
Indianapolis 44 39.45N 86.10W
Indian Ocean 27
Indonesia 27 6.00S118.00E
Indore 25 22.43N 75.50E
Indre r. 12 47.16N 0.19W
Indus r. 25 24.20N 67.47E
Inebolu 21 41.57N 33.45E
Ingende 52 0.17S 18.58E
Ingham 34 18.35S146.12E
Ingleborough mtn. 8 54.10N 2.23W
Inhambane 54 23.51S 35.29E
Inisheer i. 10 53.04N 9.32W
Inishmaan i. 10 53.06N 9.36W
Inishmore i. 10 53.08N 9.43W
Inishowen Pen. 10 55.08N 7.20W
Inishturk i. 10 53.43N 10.08W
Inner Hebrides is. 11 56.50N 6.45W
Inner Mongolia d. see Nei Monggol d. 26
Innsbruck 16 47.17N 11.25E
Interlaken 16 46.42N 7.52E
Inuvik 38 68.16N133.40W
Inuvik d. 38 68.00N130.00W
Inveraray 11 56.24N 5.05W
Inverbervie 11 56.51N 2.17W
Invercargill 29 46.26S168.21E
Inverell 37 29.46S151.10E
Invergordon 11 57.42N 4.10W
Inverness 11 57.27N 4.15W
Inverurie 11 57.17N 2.23W
Inzia r. 52 3.47S 17.57E
Ioánnina 15 39.39N 20.49E
Iona i. 11 56.20N 6.25W
Ionian Is. see Iónioi Nísoi is. 15
Ionian Sea 15 38.30N 18.45E
Iónioi Nísoi is. 15 38.45N 20.00E
Íos i. 15 36.42N 25.20E
Iowa d. 41 42.00N 93.00W
Iowa City 41 41.39N 91.30W
Ipiaú 47 14.07S 39.43W
Ipoh 27 4.36N101.02E
Ipswich Australia 37 27.38S152.40E
Ipswich U.K. 9 52.04N 1.09E
Iquitos 46 3.51S 73.13W
Iráklion 15 35.20N 25.08E
Iran 24 32.00N 54.30E
Iraq 24 33.00N 44.00E
Iringa 53 7.49S 35.39E
Irish Sea 10 53.30N 5.40W
Irkutsk 23 52.18N104.15E
Iron Gate f. 17 44.40N 22.30E
Iron Mts. 10 54.10N 7.56W
Irosin 27 12.45N124.02E
Irrapatana 36 29.03S136.28E
Irrawaddy r. 27 15.50N 95.00E
Irtysh r. 22 61.00N 68.40E
Irún 13 43.20N 1.48W
Irvine 11 55.37N 4.40W
Isangi 52 0.48N 24.03E
Isar r. 16 48.48N 12.57E
Ischia i. 14 40.43N 13.54E
Isère r. 12 45.02N 4.54E
Isfahan see Eşfahān 24
Ishim r. 22 57.50N 71.00E
Isiro 53 2.50N 27.40E
Iskenderun 21 36.37N 36.08E
Iskür r. 15 43.42N 24.27E
Isla r. 11 56.32N 3.22W
Islāmābād 25 33.40N 73.10E
Islands, B. of 29 35.15S174.15E
Islay i. 11 55.45N 6.20W
Isle of Portland f. 9 50.32N 2.25W
Isle of Wight d. 9 50.40N 1.17W
Israel 24 32.00N 35.00E
Issoire 12 45.33N 3.15E
Istanbul 24 41.02N 28.58E
Itabira 45 19.39S 43.14W
Itabuna 47 14.48S 39.18W
Itaituba 47 4.17S 55.59W
Italy 14 43.00N 12.00E
Itapetinga 47 15.17S 40.16W
Itaqui 45 29.07S 56.33W
Ithaca 44 42.26N 76.30W
Itháki 15 38.23N 20.42E
Ituiutaba 45 19.00S 49.25W
Ituri r. 53 1.45N 27.06E
Ivaí r. 45 23.20S 53.23W
Ivalo r. 18 68.43N 27.36E
Ivanhoe 36 32.56S144.22E
Ivanovo R.S.F.S.R. 20 57.00N 41.00E
Ivigtût 39 61.10N 48.00W
Ivindo 52 0.02S 12.13E
Iviza i. see Ibiza i. 13
Ivory Coast 50 7.00N 5.30W
Izmail 24 45.20N 28.50E
Izmir 24 38.24N 27.09E
Izmit 21 40.48N 29.55E

J

Jabalón r. 13 38.55N 4.07W
Jabalpur 25 23.10N 79.57E
Jaca 13 42.34N 0.33W
Jackson Mich. 44 42.15N 84.24W
Jackson Miss. 41 32.20N 90.11W
Jacksonville Fla. 41 30.20N 81.40W
Jacques Cartier, Mt. 44 49.00N 65.55W
Jacuí r. 45 29.56S 51.13W
Jaffa, C. 36 36.58S139.39E
Jaffna 25 9.38N 80.02E
Jagdalpur 25 19.04N 82.02E
Jaipur 25 26.53N 75.50E
Jakarta 27 6.08S106.45E
Jalapa 42 19.45N 96.48W
Jalón r. 13 41.47N 1.02W
Jamaica 43 18.00N 77.00W
Jamālpur 25 24.55N 89.56E
James r. S.Dak. 41 42.50N 97.15W
James B. 39 53.00N 80.00W
Jammu 25 32.42N 74.52E
Jammu & Kashmir 25 34.45N 76.00E
Jāmnagar 25 22.28N 70.04E
Jämsänkoski 19 61.55N 25.11E
Jamshedpur 25 22.48N 86.11E
Jándula r. 13 38.08N 4.08W
Janesville 41 42.42N 89.02W

59

Logroño 13 42.28N 2.26W
Loir r. 12 47.29N 0.32W
Loire r. 12 47.18N 2.00W
Loja 13 37.10N 4.09W
Loka 52 0.20N 17.57E
Lokitaung 53 4.15N 35.45E
Lokoja 50 7.49N 6.44E
Lokolo r. 52 0.45S 19.36E
Lokoro r. 52 1.40S 18.29E
Lolland i. 19 54.46N 11.30E
Lomami r. 52 0.45N 24.10E
Lomas de Zamora 49 34.46S 58.24W
Lombok i. 27 8.30S116.20E
Lomé 50 6.10N 1.21E
Lomela r. 52 0.14S 20.45E
Lomié 52 3.09N 13.35E
Lomond, Loch 11 56.07N 4.36W
Łomża 17 53.11N 22.04E
London Canada 44 42.59N 81.14W
London U.K. 9 51.32N 0.06W
Londonderry 10 55.00N 7.21W
Londonderry d. 10 55.00N 7.00W
Londonderry, C. 32 13.58S126.55E
Londrina 48 23.30S 51.13W
Long Beach town Calif. 40 33.57N118.15W
Long Eaton 8 52.54N 1.16W
Longford 10 53.44N 7.48W
Longford d. 10 53.42N 7.45W
Long I. 44 40.46N 73.00W
Long L. 44 49.29N 86.44W
Longniddry 11 55.58N 2.53W
Longreach 34 23.26S144.15E
Longtown 8 55.01N 2.58W
Lonsdale, L. 36 37.05S142.15E
Looe 9 50.51N 4.26W
Lookout, C. 41 34.34N 76.34W
Loongana 33 30.57S127.02E
Loop Head 10 52.33N 9.56W
Lopari r. 52 1.20N 20.22E
Lopez, C. 52 0.36S 8.40E
Lop Nur l. 26 40.30N 90.30E
Lorain 44 41.28N 82.11W
Loralai 25 30.22N 68.36E
Lorca 13 37.40N 1.41W
Lordsburg 40 32.22N108.43W
Lorient 12 47.45N 3.21W
Lorne 36 38.34S144.01E
Los Angeles 40 34.00N118.17W
Los Blancos 13 37.37N 0.48W
Lossiemouth 11 57.43N 3.18W
Lot r. 12 44.17N 0.22E
Lothian d. 11 55.50N 3.00W
Lotoi r. 52 1.30S 18.30E
Lotsani r. 54 22.42S 28.11E
Louangphrabang 26 19.53N102.10E
Loudéac 12 48.11N 2.45W
Loudima 52 4.06S 13.05E
Loughborough 8 52.47N 1.11W
Loughrea 10 53.12N 8.35W
Loughros More B. 10 54.48N 8.32W
Louisburgh 10 53.46N 9.49W
Louisiana d. 41 31.00N 92.30W
Louis Trichardt 54 23.03S 29.54E
Louisville Ky. 44 38.13N 85.48W
Lourdes 12 43.06N 0.02W
Louth d. 10 53.55N 6.30W
Louth 8 53.23N 0.00
Lovat r. 20 58.06N 31.37E
Lovech 15 43.08N 24.44E
Lovoi r. 53 8.14S 26.40E
Lovua r. 52 6.08S 20.35E
Lowa r. Kivu 52 1.25S 25.55E
Lowell 44 42.39N 71.18W
Lower Hutt 29 41.13S174.55E
Lower Lough Erne 10 54.28N 7.48W
Lowestoft 9 52.29N 1.44E
Łowicz 17 52.06N 19.55E
Loxton 36 34.38S140.38E
Loyauté, Îles is. 30 21.00S167.00E
Luachimo r. 52 6.32S 20.57E
Luama r. 53 4.45S 26.55E
Luanda 52 8.50S 13.20E
Luanginga r. 52 15.11S 23.05E
Luangwa r. Central 53 15.32S 30.28E
Luanshya 53 13.09S 28.24E
Luao 52 10.41S 22.09E
Luapula r. 53 9.25S 28.36E
Luarca 13 43.33N 6.31W
Lubango 52 14.52S 13.30E
Lubao 52 5.19S 25.43E
Lubbock 40 33.35N101.53W
Lübeck 16 53.52N 10.40E
Lubefu r. 52 4.05S 23.00E
Lubilash r. 52 4.59S 23.25E
Lublin 17 51.18N 22.31E
Lubudi 52 9.57S 25.59E
Lubudi r. K.Occidental 52 4.00S 21.23E
Lubudi r. Shaba 52 9.13S 25.40E
Lubumbashi 53 11.44S 27.29E
Lubutu 52 0.48S 26.19E
Luce B. 11 54.45N 4.47W
Lucena 13 37.25N 4.29W
Lučenec 17 48.20N 19.40E
Lucero 42 30.50N106.30W
Luckenwalde 16 52.05N 13.11E
Lucknow 25 26.51N 80.55E
Lüda 26 38.49N121.48E
Lüderitz 54 26.37S 15.09E
Ludhiāna 25 30.55N 75.51E
Ludington 44 43.58N 86.27W
Ludlow 9 52.23N 2.42W
Ludvika 19 60.09N 15.11E
Ludwigshafen 16 49.29N 8.27E
Luebo 52 5.16S 21.27E
Luengue r. 52 16.58S 21.15E
Lufeng 26 23.01N115.35E
Lufira r. 52 8.15S 26.30E
Lufkin 41 31.21N 94.47W
Luga 20 58.42N 29.49E
Lugano 12 46.01N 8.57E
Lugenda r. 53 11.23S 38.30E
Lugh Ganane 53 3.56N 42.32E
Lugnaquilla Mtn. 10 52.58N 6.28W
Lugo 13 43.00N 7.33W
Lugoj 17 45.42N 21.56E
Luiana r. 52 17.28S 23.02E
Luilaka r. 52 0.15S 19.00E
Luilu r. 52 6.22S 23.53E
Luiro r. 18 67.18N 27.28E
Luisa 52 7.15S 22.27E
Lukala 52 5.23S 13.02E
Lukanga Swamp f. 53 14.15S 27.30E
Lukenie r. 52 2.43S 18.12E
Lukuga r. 53 5.37S 26.58E
Lukula r. 52 4.15S 17.59E
Luleå 18 65.34N 22.10E
Lulonga r. 52 0.42N 18.26E
Lulua r. 52 5.03S 21.07E
Lumsden 29 45.44S168.26E
Lund 19 55.42N 13.11E
Lundazi 53 12.19S 33.11E
Lundi r. 54 21.20S 32.23E
Lundy i. 9 51.10N 4.41W
Lune r. 8 54.03N 2.49W
Lüneburg 16 53.15N 10.24E
Lunga r. 52 14.28S 26.27E
Lungwebungu r. 52 14.20S 23.15E
Luofo 53 0.12S 29.15E
Luoyang 26 34.48N112.25E
Lurgan 10 54.28N 6.21W
Lurio 53 13.30S 40.30E
Lurio r. 53 13.32S 40.31E
Lusaka 53 15.20S 28.14E
Lusambo 52 4.59S 23.26E
Lushoto 53 4.48S 38.20E
Lusk 40 42.47N104.26W
Luton 9 51.53N 0.25W
Lutsk 17 50.42N 25.15E
Lutterworth 9 52.28N 1.12W
Luvua r. 53 6.45S 27.00E
Luwegu r. 53 8.30S 37.28E
Luwingu 53 10.13S 30.05E
Luxembourg 16 49.50N 6.15E
Luxembourg town 16 49.37N 6.08E
Luxor see Al Uqşur 51
Luzern 16 47.03N 8.17E
Luzhou 26 28.48N105.23E
Luziânia 47 16.18S 47.57W
Luzon i. 27 17.50N121.00E
Lvov 17 49.50N 24.00E
Lybster 11 58.18N 3.18W
Lycksele 18 64.36N 18.40E
Lydenburg 54 25.06S 30.27E
Lyme B. 9 50.40N 2.55W
Lyme Regis 9 50.44N 2.57W
Lymington 9 50.46N 1.32W
Lyndhurst 36 30.19S138.24E
Lynn 44 42.28N 70.57W
Lynn Lake town 39 56.51N101.01W
Lynton 9 51.14N 3.50W
Lyon 12 45.46N 4.50E
Lyons r. 32 25.02S115.09E
Lysekil 19 58.16N 11.26E
Lytham St. Anne's 8 53.45N 3.01W
Lyubertsy 20 55.38N 37.58E

M

Maamakeogh mtn. 10 54.17N 9.29W
Maamturk Mts. 10 53.32N 9.42W
Ma'ān 24 30.11N 35.43E
Maas r. 16 51.44N 4.42E
Maastricht 16 50.51N 5.42E
Mabel Creek town 35 29.01S134.17E
Mablethorpe 8 53.21N 0.14E
Macalister r. 37 37.55S146.50E
Macapá 47 0.04N 51.04W
Macaroni 34 16.36S141.30E
Macau 26 22.11N113.33E
Macclesfield 8 53.16N 2.09W
Macdonald, L. 32 23.30S129.00E
Macdonnell Ranges mts. 34 23.45S133.20E
Macduff 11 57.40N 2.29W
Macedon mtn. 37 37.27S144.34E
Maceió 47 9.40S 35.44W
Macerata 14 43.18N 13.30E
Macfarlane, L. 36 31.55S136.42E
Macgillycuddy's Reeks mts. 10 52.00N 9.43W
Machattie, L. 34 24.50S139.48E
Macheke 54 18.08S 31.49E
Machrihanish 11 55.25N 5.44W
Machynlleth 9 52.35N 3.51W
Macintyre r. 37 28.50S150.50E
Mackay, L. 32 22.30S149.10E
Mackenzie Australia 34 22.48S149.15E
Mackenzie Canada 38 69.20N134.00W
Mackenzie Mts. 38 64.00N130.00W
Mackinnon Road town 53 3.50S 39.03E
Maclear 54 31.04S 28.21E
Macleay r. 37 30.52S153.01E
Macomer 14 40.16N 8.45E
Mâcon 12 46.18N 4.50E
Macon Ga. 41 32.47N 83.37W
Macpherson Range mts. 37 28.15S153.00E
Macquarie r. 37 30.07S147.24E
Macquarie Marshes 37 30.50S147.32E
Macroom 10 51.54N 8.58W
Macumba r. 35 27.55S137.15E
Madagascar 3 17.00S 46.00E
Madawaska 44 47.21N 68.20W
Madeira i. 50 32.45N 17.00W
Madeira r. 46 3.20S 59.00W
Madeira, Arquipélago da is. 50 32.40N 16.45W
Madeleine, Îles de la is. 39 47.30N 61.45W
Madhya Pradesh d. 25 23.30N 78.30E
Madison Wisc. 41 43.04N 89.22W
Mado Gashi 53 0.40N 39.11E
Madras 25 13.05N 80.18E
Madre del Sur, Sierra mts. 42 17.00N100.00W
Madrid 13 40.25N 3.43W
Madukani 53 3.57S 35.49E
Madura i. 27 7.02S113.22E
Madurai 25 9.55N 78.07E
Maestra, Sierra mts. 43 20.10N 76.30W
Mafeteng 54 29.51S 27.13E
Mafia I. 53 7.50S 39.50E
Mafikeng 54 25.52S 25.36E
Magadi 53 1.53S 36.18E
Magallanes, Estrecho de str. 49 53.00S 71.00W
Magalluf 13 39.30N 2.31E
Magangué 46 9.14N 74.46W
Magdalena r. 46 10.56N 74.58W
Magdeburg 16 52.08N 11.36E
Magellan's Str. see Magallanes, Estrecho de str. 49
Magerøya i. 18 71.03N 25.45E
Maggiore, Lago l. 14 46.00N 8.40E
Magherafelt 10 54.45N 6.38W
Magnitogorsk 20 53.28N 59.06E
Magué 53 15.46S 31.42E
Mahadday Weyne 53 2.58N 45.32E
Mahagi 53 2.16N 30.59E
Mahalapye 54 23.04S 26.47E
Mahārāshtra d. 25 19.40N 76.00E
Mahdia 46 5.10N 59.12W
Mahia Pen. 29 39.10S177.50E
Mahón 13 39.55N 4.18E
Maidenhead 9 51.32N 0.44W
Maidstone 9 51.17N 0.32E
Maiduguri 50 11.53N 13.16E
Maiko r. 52 0.15N 25.35E
Main r. 16 50.00N 8.19E
Main Barrier Range mts. 36 31.25S141.25E
Mai Ndombe l. 52 2.00S 18.20E
Maine d. 44 45.15N 69.15W
Mainland i. Orkney Is. 11 59.00N 3.10W
Mainz 16 50.00N 8.16E
Maípo mtn. 49 34.10S 69.50W
Maitland N.S.W. 37 32.33S151.33E
Majene 27 3.33S118.59E
Majorca i. see Mallorca i. 13
Majuba Hill 54 27.26S 29.48E
Makarikari Salt Pan f. 54 20.50S 25.45E
Makasar, Selat str. 27 3.00S118.00E
Makeyevka 21 48.01N 38.00E
Makhachkala 21 42.59N 47.30E
Makkah 24 21.26N 39.49E
Makó 17 46.13N 20.30E
Makran f. 24 26.30N 61.20E
Makurdi 50 7.44N 8.35E
Malabo 52 3.45N 8.48E
Malacca, Str. of 27 3.00N100.30E
Málaga 13 36.43N 4.25W
Malakâl 51 9.31N 31.40E
Malakand 25 34.34N 71.56E
Malanje 52 9.36S 16.21E
Mälaren l. 19 59.30N 17.12E
Malatya 21 38.22N 38.18E
Malaŵi 53 12.00S 34.00E
Malaŵi, L. 53 12.00S 34.30E
Malaysia 27 5.00N110.00E
Malbork 17 54.02N 19.01E
Maldives 24 6.20N 73.00E
Maldon 9 51.43N 0.41E
Maldonado 45 34.57S 54.59W
Maléa, Ákra c. 15 36.27N 23.11E
Malebo Pool f. 52 4.15S 15.25E
Malema 53 14.55S 37.09E
Mali 50 16.00N 3.00W
Malindi 53 3.14S 40.08E
Malin Head 10 55.23N 7.24W
Malin More 10 54.42N 8.48W
Mallacoota Inlet b. 37 37.34S149.43E
Mallaig 11 57.00N 5.50W
Mallorca i. 13 39.35N 3.00E
Mallow 10 52.08N 8.39W
Malmesbury 54 33.28S 18.43E
Malmö 19 55.36N 13.00E
Malone 44 44.51N 74.17W
Malonga 52 10.26S 23.10E
Malpas 36 34.44S140.43E
Malta 14 35.55N 14.25E
Maltby 8 53.25N 1.12W
Malton 8 54.09N 0.48W
Mambasa 53 1.20N 29.05E
Mambilima Falls town 53 10.32S 28.45E
Mamore r. 48 12.00S 65.15W
Mamuju 27 2.21S118.55E
Man 50 7.31N 7.37W
Man, Isle of 8 54.15N 4.30W
Manacor 13 39.32N 3.12E
Manado 27 1.30N124.58E
Managua 43 12.06N 86.18W
Managua, Lago de l. 43 12.10N 86.30W
Manapouri, L. 29 45.30S167.00E
Manaus 46 3.06S 60.00W
Manchester 8 53.30N 2.15W
Manchurian Plain f. see Dongbei Pingyuan f. 26
Mandal 19 58.02N 7.27E
Mandalay 26 21.58N 96.04E
Mandalgovi 26 45.40N106.10E
Mandeb, Bāb el Str. 24 13.00N 43.10E
Mandurah 33 32.31S115.41E
Manfred 36 33.21S143.50E
Manfredonia, Golfo di g. 14 41.35N 16.05E
Mangalia 17 43.50N 28.35E
Mangalore 25 12.54N 74.51E
Mangaweka 29 39.48S175.48E
Mangnai 26 37.52N 91.26E
Mango 50 10.23N 0.30E
Mangochi 53 14.29S 35.15E
Manhiça 54 25.24S 32.49E
Maniamba 53 12.30S 35.05E
Manica 54 19.00S 33.00E
Manila 27 14.36N120.59E
Manildra 37 33.12S148.41E
Maningrida 34 12.03S134.13E
Manipur d. 25 25.00N 93.40E
Manisa 15 38.37N 27.28E
Manistee r. 44 44.14N 86.20W
Manitoba d. 39 54.00N 96.00W
Manitoba, L. 39 51.35N 99.00W
Manitoulin I. 44 45.45N 82.30W
Manizales 46 5.03N 75.32W
Manjimup 33 34.14S116.06E
Manly 37 33.47S151.17E
Mann r. 34 12.20S134.07E
Mannahill 36 32.26S139.59E
Mannar, G. of 25 8.20N 79.00E
Mannheim 16 49.30N 8.28E
Mannin B. 10 53.28N 10.06W
Mannum 36 34.50S139.20E
Manokwari 27 0.53S134.05E
Manono 53 7.18S 27.24E
Manorhamilton 10 54.18N 8.10W
Manresa 13 41.43N 1.50E
Mansa 53 11.10S 28.52E
Mansel I. 39 62.00N 80.00W
Mansfield 8 53.08N 1.12W
Mantova 14 45.09N 10.47E
Mänttä 19 62.02N 24.38E
Manukau Harbour est. 29 37.10S174.00E
Manus i. 30 2.05S147.00E
Manyara, L. 53 3.40S 35.50E
Manych r. 21 47.14N 40.20E
Manyinga r. 52 13.28S 24.25E
Manyoni 53 5.46S 34.50E
Manzanares 13 39.00N 3.23W
Manzanillo 43 20.21N 77.21W
Manzhouli 26 49.36N117.28E
Manzini 54 26.29S 31.24E
Maoke, Pegunungan mts. 27 4.00S137.30E
Maoming 26 21.50N110.58E
Mapai 54 22.51S 32.00E
Mappi 27 7.06S139.23E
Maputo 54 25.58S 32.35E
Maquela do Zombo 52 6.06S 15.12E
Mar, Serra do mts. 45 23.00S 44.40W
Mara r. 53 1.30S 33.52E
Maracaibo 46 10.44N 71.37W
Maracaju, Serra de mts. 45 21.38S 55.10W
Maracay 46 10.20N 67.28W
Maradi 50 13.29N 7.10E
Marahuaca, Cerro mtn. 46 3.37N 65.25W
Marajó, Ilha de i. 47 1.00S 49.40W
Maralal 53 1.15N 36.48E
Maramba 52 17.40S 25.50E
Maranoa r. 35 27.55S148.30E
Marão 54 24.21S 34.07E
Marathón 15 38.10N 23.59E
Marbella 13 36.31N 4.53W
Marble Bar 32 21.16S119.45E
Marburg 16 50.49N 8.36E
March 9 52.33N 0.05E
Marchant Hill 36 32.16S138.49E
Mar Chiquita l. 48 30.42S 62.36W
Mardan 25 34.12N 72.02E
Mar del Plata 49 38.00S 57.32W
Marden 9 51.11N 0.30E
Mardie 32 21.14S115.57E
Mardin 21 37.19N 40.43E
Maree, Loch 11 57.41N 5.28W
Mareeba 34 17.00S145.26E
Marettimo i. 14 37.58N 12.05E
Margaret r. 36 29.26S137.00E
Margarita, Isla de i. 46 11.00N 64.00W
Margate 9 51.23N 1.24E
Maria I. 34 14.52S135.40E
Mariana Is. 30 16.00N145.30E
Marianao 43 23.03N 82.29W
Marie-Galante i. 43 15.54N 61.11W
Mariental 54 24.38S 17.58E
Mariestad 19 58.43N 13.51E
Marília 45 22.13S 50.20W
Maringá 45 23.36S 52.02W
Marínga r. 52 1.13N 19.50E
Maringue 54 17.55S 34.24E
Marinha Grande 13 39.45N 8.55W
Mariscal Estigarribia 45 22.03S 60.35W
Maritsa r. 15 41.00N 26.15E
Market Drayton 8 52.55N 2.30W
Market Harborough 9 52.29N 0.55W
Market Rasen 8 53.24N 0.20W
Market Weighton 8 53.52N 0.04W
Markha r. 23 63.37N119.00E
Marlborough d. 29 41.40S173.40E
Marlborough 9 51.26N 1.44W
Marmara i. 15 40.38N 27.37E
Marmara, Sea of see Marmara Denizi sea 15
Marmara Denizi sea 15 40.45N 28.15E
Marmaris 15 36.50N 28.17E
Marne r. 12 48.50N 2.25E
Marnoo 36 36.40S142.55E
Maroua 50 10.35N 14.20E
Marquard 54 28.39S 27.25E
Marquesas Is. see Marquises, Îles is. 31
Marquises, Îles is. 31 9.00S139.30W
Marra r. 37 30.05S147.05E
Marrakech 50 31.49N 8.00W
Marree 36 29.40S138.04E
Marrupa 53 13.10S 37.30E
Marsabit 53 2.20N 37.59E
Marsala 14 37.48N 12.27E
Marsden 37 33.46S147.35E
Marseille 12 43.18N 5.22E
Marshall Tex. 41 32.33N 94.22W
Marshall Is. 30 10.00N172.00E
Martaban, G. of 27 15.10N 96.30E
Martés, Sierra mts. 13 39.10N 1.00W
Martha's Vineyard i. 44 41.25N 70.40W
Martigny 16 46.07N 7.05E
Martinique i. 43 14.40N 61.00W
Martin Pt. 38 70.10N143.50W
Marton 29 40.04S175.25E
Mary Kathleen 34 20.49S140.00E
Maryland d. 44 39.00N 76.45W
Maryport 8 54.43N 3.30W
Masai Steppe f. 53 4.30S 37.00E
Masaka 53 0.20S 31.46E
Masasi 53 10.43S 38.48E
Masbate i. 27 12.00N123.30E
Maseru 54 29.18S 27.28E
Mashhad 24 36.16N 59.34E
Mashonaland f. 54 18.20S 32.00E
Masi-Manimba 52 4.47S 17.54E
Masindi 53 1.41N 31.45E
Maşīrah i. 24 20.30N 58.50E
Mask, Lough 10 53.38N 9.22W
Mason City 41 43.10N 93.10W
Masqaţ 24 23.36N 58.37E
Massachusetts d. 44 42.15N 71.50W
Massangena 54 21.31S 33.03E
Massif Central mts. 12 45.00N 3.30E
Massinga 54 23.20S 35.25E
Masterton 29 40.57S175.39E
Masvingo 54 20.10S 30.49E
Matabeleland f. 54 19.50S 28.15E
Matadi 52 5.50S 13.36E
Matagorda B. 41 28.30N 96.20W
Matakana I. 29 37.35S176.15E
Matam 50 15.40N 13.15W
Matamata 29 37.49S175.46E
Matamoros Tamaulipas 42 25.50N 97.31W
Matandu r. 53 8.44S 39.22E
Matanzas 43 23.04N 81.35W
Mataura r. 29 46.34S168.45E
Matawai 29 38.21S177.32E
Matehuala 42 23.40N100.40W
Matlock 8 53.09N 1.32W
Mato Grosso town 48 15.05S 59.57W
Mato Grosso, Planalto do f. 48 16.00S 54.00W
Matope 53 15.20S 34.57E
Matopo Hills 54 20.45S 28.30E
Matsue 26 35.29N133.00E
Matsusaka 28 34.34N136.32E
Matsuyama 26 33.50N132.47E
Mattagami r. 44 50.43N 81.29W
Matterhorn mtn. 12 45.58N 7.38E
Maude 36 34.27S144.21E
Maui i. Hawaii 40 20.45N156.15W
Maumere 27 8.35S122.13E
Maun 54 19.52S 23.40E
Mauna Loa mtn. 31 19.29N155.36W
Mauritania 50 20.00N 10.00W
Mavinga 52 15.47S 20.21E
Mawlaik 26 23.50N 94.30E
Maya i. 27 1.09S109.45E
Maya 13 43.12N 1.29W
Mayaguana I. 43 22.30N 73.00W
Mayagüez 43 18.13N 67.09W
Maya Mts. 43 16.30N 89.00W
Maybole 11 55.21N 4.41W
Mayenne 12 48.18N 0.37W
Mayenne r. 12 47.30N 0.37W
Maykop 21 44.37N 40.48E
Mayo d. 10 53.47N 9.07W
Mayo, Plains of f. 10 53.46N 9.05W
Mayo Landing 38 63.45N135.45W
Mayor I. 29 37.15S176.15E
Mayotte, Île i. 53 12.50S 45.10E
Mayumba 52 3.23S 10.38E
Mazabuka 53 15.50S 27.47E
Mazatenango 42 14.31N 91.30W
Mazatlán 42 23.11N106.25W
Mažeikiai 19 56.19N 22.20E
Mazowe r. 54 16.32S 33.25E
Mazowe 54 17.30S 30.58E
Mbabane 54 26.19S 31.08E
M'Baiki 52 3.53N 18.01E
Mbala 53 8.50S 31.24E
Mbale 53 1.04N 34.12E
Mbanza Congo 52 6.18S 14.16E
Mbarara 53 0.36S 30.40E
Mbeya 53 8.54S 33.29E
Mbinda 52 2.11S 12.55E
M'bridge r. 52 7.12S 12.55E
Mbuji Mayi 52 6.08S 23.39E
Mbulamuti 53 0.50N 33.05E
McArthur r. 34 15.54S136.40E
McClintock Channel 39 71.20N102.00W
McClure Str. 38 74.30N116.00W
McConaughy, L. 40 41.20N102.00W
McCook 40 40.15N100.45W
McGrath 38 62.58N155.40W
Mchinja 53 9.44S 39.45E
Mchinji 53 13.48S 32.55E
McIlwraith Range mts. 34 14.00S143.10E
McKeesport 44 40.21N 79.52W
McKinley, Mt. 38 63.00N151.00W
Meath d. 10 53.32N 6.40W
Meaux 12 48.58N 2.54E
Mecca see Makkah 24
Meconta 53 15.00S 39.50E
Medan 27 3.35N 98.39E
Mededsiz mtn. 21 37.33N 34.38E
Medellín 46 6.15N 75.36W
Médenine 50 33.24N 10.25E
Mederdra 50 16.55N 15.39W
Medford Oreg. 40 42.20N122.52W
Medicine Hat 38 50.03N110.41W
Medina see Al Madīnah 24
Medina del Campo 13 41.20N 4.55W
Medina de Ríoseco 13 41.53N 5.03W
Mediterranean Sea 50 37.00N 15.00E
Medveditsa r. 21 49.35N 42.45E
Medway r. 9 51.24N 0.31E
Meekatharra 32 26.35S118.30E
Meerut 25 28.59N 77.42E
Mégara 15 38.00N 23.21E
Meghalaya d. 25 25.30N 91.00E
Meiktila 26 20.53N 95.50E
Meiningen 16 50.34N 10.25E
Meissen 16 51.10N 13.28E
Meknès 50 33.53N 5.37W
Mekong r. 27 10.00N106.40E
Melanesia is. 30 5.00N165.00E
Melbourne 37 37.45S144.58E
Melfi 14 40.59N 15.39E
Melilla 13 35.17N 2.57W
Melitopol 21 46.51N 35.22E
Mellerud 19 58.42N 12.28E
Melmore Pt. 10 55.15N 7.49W
Melo 45 32.22S 54.10W
Melrose 11 55.36N 2.43W
Melton Mowbray 8 52.46N 0.53W
Melun 12 48.32N 2.40E
Melvich 11 58.33N 3.55W
Melville B. 34 12.10S136.32E
Melville I. 34 11.30S131.00E
Melville Pen. 39 68.00N 84.00W
Melvin, Lough 10 54.26N 8.12W
Memba 53 14.16S 40.30E
Memmingen 16 47.59N 10.11E
Memphis Tenn. 41 35.05N 90.00W
Menai Str. 8 53.17N 4.20W
Mendawai r. 27 3.17S113.20E
Mende 12 44.32N 3.30E
Mendip Hills 9 51.15N 2.40W
Mendocino, C. 40 40.26N124.24W
Mendoza 49 32.54S 68.50W
Menindee 36 32.23S142.30E
Menongue 52 14.40S 17.41E
Menorca i. 13 40.00N 4.00E
Mentawai, Kepulauan is. 27 2.50S 99.00E
Menton 12 43.47N 7.30E
Menzies 33 29.41S121.02E
Meppel 16 52.42N 6.12E
Meppen 16 52.41N 7.17E
Merano 14 46.41N 11.10E
Merauke 27 8.30S140.22E
Merbein 36 34.11S142.04E
Merced 40 37.17N120.29W
Mere 9 51.05N 2.16W
Meredith 36 37.50S144.05E
Mergui 27 12.26N 98.38E
Mergui Archipelago is. 27 11.15N 98.00E
Meribah 36 34.42S140.53E
Mérida 43 20.59N 89.39W
Meridian 41 32.21N 88.42W
Merino 36 37.45S141.35E
Merrick mtn. 11 55.08N 4.29W
Mersea I. 9 51.47N 0.58E
Merseburg 16 51.22N 12.00E
Mersey r. 8 53.22N 2.37W
Merseyside d. 8 53.28N 3.00W
Mersin 21 36.47N 34.37E
Mersing 27 2.25N103.50E
Merthyr Tydfil 9 51.45N 3.23W
Merton 9 51.25N 0.12W
Meru mtn. 53 3.15S 36.44E
Merzifon 21 40.52N 35.28E
Mesolóngion 15 38.23N 21.23E
Mesopotamia f. 24 33.30N 44.30E
Messalo r. 53 11.38S 40.27E
Messina 14 38.13N 15.34E
Messini 15 37.03N 22.00E
Messiniakós, Kólpos g. 15 36.50N 22.05E
Mesta r. Bulgaria see Néstos r. 15
Meta r. 46 6.10N 67.30W
Metković 15 43.03N 17.38E
Metz 12 49.07N 6.11E
Meuse r. Belgium see Maas r. 16
Mexicali 42 32.26N115.30W
Mexico 42 20.00N100.00W
Mexico, G. of 42 25.00N 90.00W
Mexico City see Ciudad de México 42
Mezen r. 20 65.50N 44.18E
Miami Fla. 41 25.45N 80.10W
Mianyang Sichuan 26 31.26N104.45E
Miass 22 55.00N 60.00E
Michigan d. 44 44.00N 85.00W
Michigan, L. 44 44.00N 87.00W
Michigan City 44 41.43N 86.54W
Michurinsk 20 52.54N 40.30E
Micronesia is. 30 8.00N160.00E
Middle I. 33 34.07S123.12E
Middlesbrough 8 54.34N 1.13W
Middletown Ind. 44 39.31N 84.13W
Mid Glamorgan d. 9 51.38N 3.25W
Midland Mich. 44 43.38N 84.14W
Midleton 10 51.55N 8.10W
Midway Is. 30 28.15N177.25W
Midye 15 41.37N 28.07E
Mieres 13 43.15N 5.46W
Mijares r. 13 39.58N 0.01W
Mikhaylovka 21 50.05N 43.15E
Miki 28 34.48N134.59E
Mikindani 53 10.16S 40.05E
Mikkeli 20 61.44N 27.15E
Míkonos i. 15 37.29N 25.25E
Mikumi 53 7.22S 37.00E
Milan see Milano 14
Milange 53 16.09S 35.44E
Milano 14 45.28N 9.10E
Milâs 24 37.18N 27.48E
Mildenhall 9 52.20N 0.30E
Mildura 36 34.14S142.13E
Miles City 40 46.24N105.48W
Milford Haven town 9 51.43N 5.02W
Milford Sound town 29 44.41S167.56E
Miling 33 30.27S116.20E
Milk r. 40 47.55N106.15W
Millau 12 44.06N 3.05E
Miller r. 36 30.05S136.07E
Millerovo 21 48.55N 40.25E
Milleur Pt. 11 55.01N 5.07W
Millicent 36 37.36S140.22E
Millom 8 54.13N 3.16W
Mílos i. 15 36.40N 24.26E
Milparinka 36 29.45S141.55E
Milton Keynes 9 52.03N 0.42W
Milwaukee 41 43.03N 87.56W
Minas 49 34.23S 55.14W
Minatitlán 42 17.59N 94.32W
Mindanao i. 27 7.30N125.00E
Mindarie 36 34.51S140.12E
Minden 16 52.18N 8.54E
Mindoro i. 27 13.00N121.00E
Mindra mtn. 17 45.20N 23.32E
Minehead 9 51.12N 3.29W
Minerva 34 24.00S148.05E
Mingary 36 32.09S140.46E
Mingela 34 19.53S146.40E
Mingenew 33 29.11S115.26E
Minigwal, L. 33 29.35S123.12E
Minneapolis 41 45.00N 93.15W
Minnesota d. 41 46.00N 95.00W
Minnipa 36 32.51S135.09E
Miño r. 13 41.50N 8.52W
Minorca i. see Menorca i. 13
Minsk 17 53.51N 27.30E
Miranda de Ebro 13 42.41N 2.57W
Miranda do Douro 13 41.30N 6.16W
Mirande 12 43.31N 0.25E
Mirandela 13 41.28N 7.10W
Mirecourt 12 48.18N 6.08E
Mirim, L. 45 33.10S 53.30W
Mirpur Khās 25 25.33N 69.05E
Mirzāpur 25 25.09N 82.35E
Misoöl i. 27 1.50S130.10E
Mississippi d. 41 33.00N 90.00W
Mississippi r. 41 28.55N 89.05W
Missoula 40 46.52N114.00W
Missouri d. 41 39.00N 93.00W
Missouri r. 41 38.40N 90.20W
Mistassini, Lac l. 44 51.15N 73.10W
Mitchell r. N.S.W. 37 29.40S152.18E
Mitchell r. Qld. 34 15.12S141.35E
Mitchell r. Vic. 37 37.53S147.41E
Mitchell, Mt. 41 35.57N 82.16W
Mitchelstown 10 52.16N 8.17W
Mittagong 37 34.27S150.25E
Mitumba, Monts mts. 53 3.00S 28.30E
Mitwaba 53 8.32S 27.20E
Mitzic 52 0.48N 11.30E
Miyakonojō 26 31.43N131.02E
Mizen Head 10 51.27N 9.50W
Mizoram d. 25 23.40N 92.40E
Mjölby 19 58.19N 15.08E
Mjösa l. 19 60.40N 11.00E
Mkushi 53 13.40S 29.26E
Mladá Boleslav 16 50.26N 14.55E
Mljet i. 15 42.45N 17.30E
Moamba 54 25.35S 32.13E
Moanda 52 1.25S 13.18E
Moatize 53 16.10S 33.40E
Moba 53 7.03S 29.42E
Mobile 41 30.40N 88.05W
Mobridge 40 45.31N100.25W
Moçambique town 53 15.00S 40.47E
Mocimboa da Praia 53 11.19S 40.19E
Mocuba 53 16.52S 37.02E
Modane 12 45.12N 6.40E
Modder r. 54 29.03S 23.56E
Modena 14 44.39N 10.55E
Modica 14 36.51N 14.51E
Moffat 11 55.20N 3.27W
Mogadisho 53 2.02N 45.21E
Mogilev 17 53.54N 30.20E
Mogincual 53 15.33S 40.29E
Mogok 25 23.00N 96.30E
Mohéli i. 53 12.22S 43.45E
Mohoro 53 8.09S 39.07E
Mo-i-Rana 18 66.19N 14.10E
Moisie r. 39 50.13N 66.02W
Moissac 12 44.07N 1.05E
Mokp'o 26 34.50N126.25E
Mold 8 53.10N 3.08W
Molde 18 62.44N 7.08E
Molepolole 54 24.26S 25.34E
Molfetta 15 41.12N 16.36E
Molina de Aragón 13 40.50N 1.54W
Moline 41 41.31N 90.26W
Moliro 53 8.11S 30.29E
Mölndal 19 57.39N 12.01E
Molodechno 17 54.16N 26.50E
Molokai i. Hawaii 40 21.20N157.00W
Molopo r. 54 28.30S 20.22E
Molteno 54 31.23S 26.21E
Moluccas is. 27 4.00S128.00E
Moma 53 16.40S 39.10E
Mombasa 53 4.04S 39.40E
Mön i. 19 55.00N 12.20E
Mona i. 43 18.06N 67.54W
Monaco 12 43.40N 7.25E
Monadhliath Mts. 11 57.09N 4.08W
Monaghan 10 54.15N 6.58W
Monaghan d. 10 54.10N 7.00W
Monchegorsk 20 67.55N 33.01E
Mönchen-Gladbach 16 51.12N 6.25E
Monclova 42 26.55N101.20W
Moncton 39 46.06N 64.50W
Mondovì 14 44.24N 7.50E
Monforte 13 42.32N 7.30W
Monga 51 4.05N 22.56E
Mongala r. 52 1.58N 19.55E
Mongolia 26 46.30N104.00E
Mongu 52 15.10S 23.09E
Monifieth 11 56.29N 2.50W
Monkoto 52 1.39S 20.41E
Monmouth 9 51.48N 2.43W
Monroe La. 41 32.31N 92.06W
Monrovia 50 6.20N 10.46W
Mons 16 50.27N 3.57E
Montana d. 40 47.00N110.00W
Montargis 12 48.00N 2.44E
Montauban 12 44.01N 1.20E
Montbrison 12 45.37N 4.04E
Mont Cenis, Col du pass 12 45.15N 6.55E
Mont de Marsan town 12 43.54N 0.30W
Monte Azul town 45 15.53S 42.53W
Monte Carlo 12 43.44N 7.25E
Montecristo i. 14 42.20N 10.19E
Montego Bay town 43 18.27N 77.56W
Montélimar 12 44.33N 4.45E
Monterey B. 40 36.45N122.00W
Montería 46 8.45N 75.54W
Montero 48 17.20S 63.15W
Monterrey 42 25.40N100.20W
Monte Santu, Capo di c. 14 40.05N 9.44E
Montes Claros 45 16.45S 43.52W
Montevideo 49 34.53S 56.11W
Montgomery Ala. 41 32.22N 86.20W
Montijo 13 38.42N 8.59W
Montluçon 12 46.20N 2.36E
Montmagny 44 46.56N 70.28W
Montmédy 12 49.31N 5.21E
Montmorillon 12 46.26N 0.52E
Montoro 13 38.02N 4.23W
Montpellier 12 43.36N 3.53E
Montreal 44 45.30N 73.36W
Montreal r. 44 47.14N 84.39W
Montrejeau 12 43.05N 0.33E
Montreuil 12 50.28N 1.46E
Montreux 16 46.27N 6.55E
Montrose 11 56.43N 2.29W
Montsant, Sierra de mts. 13 41.20N 1.00E
Montserrat i. 43 16.45N 62.14W
Monywa 26 22.05N 95.15E
Monza 14 45.35N 9.16E
Monze 53 16.16S 27.28E
Monzón 13 41.52N 0.10E
Moora 33 30.40S116.01E
Moore, L. 33 29.30S117.30E
Moorfoot Hills 11 55.43N 3.03W
Moorhead 41 46.51N 96.44W
Moosehead L. 44 45.40N 69.40W
Moose Jaw 38 50.23N105.35W
Mootwingee 36 31.52S141.14E
Mopti 50 14.29N 4.10W
Morādābād 25 28.50N 78.47E
Moralana 36 31.42S138.12E
Morar, Loch 11 56.56N 4.00W
Moray Firth est. 11 57.35N 5.15W
Morecambe 8 54.03N 2.52W
Morelia 42 19.40N101.11W
Morella 13 40.37N 0.06W
Morena, Sierra mts. 13 38.10N 5.00W
Moreton I. 35 27.10S153.25E
Morez 12 46.31N 6.02E
Morgan 36 34.02S139.40E
Morgan City 41 29.41N 91.13W
Morkalla 36 34.22S141.10E
Morlaix 12 48.35N 3.50W
Mornington I. 34 16.33S139.24E
Morocco 50 31.00N 5.00W
Morogoro 53 6.47S 37.40E
Moroni 53 11.40S 43.19E
Morotai i. 27 2.10N128.30E
Moroto 53 2.32N 34.41E
Morpeth 8 55.10N 1.40W
Morrinsville 29 37.39S175.32E
Mortagne 12 48.32N 0.33E
Mortlake town 36 38.05S142.48E
Morundah 37 34.56S146.18E
Morven 34 26.25S147.05E
Morvern f. 11 56.37N 5.45W
Moscow see Moskva 20
Mosel r. 16 50.23N 7.37E
Mosgiel 29 45.53S170.22E
Moshi 53 3.20S 37.21E
Mosjöen 18 65.50N 13.10E
Moskva 20 55.45N 37.42E
Moskva r. 20 55.08N 38.50E
Mosquitos, Costa de f. 43 13.00N 84.00W
Moss 19 59.26N 10.42E
Mossaka 52 1.20S 16.44E
Mossburn 29 45.41S168.15E
Mossgiel 37 33.18S144.05E
Mossman 34 16.28S145.22E
Mossoró 47 5.10S 37.18W
Most 16 50.31N 13.39E
Mostar 15 43.20N 17.50E
Motagua r. 43 15.56N 87.45W
Motala 19 58.33N 15.03E
Motherwell 11 55.48N 4.00W
Mouila 52 1.50S 11.02E
Moulamein 36 35.03S144.05E
Moulins 12 46.34N 3.20E
Moulmein 27 16.55N 97.49E
Moundou 50 8.34N 16.05E
Mountain Ash 9 51.42N 3.22W
Mount Barker town W.A. 33 34.36S117.37E
Mount Bellew town 10 53.28N 8.30W
Mount Darwin town 53 16.46S 31.36E
Mount Douglas town 34 21.31S146.50E
Mount Eba town 36 30.12S135.33E
Mount Fletcher town 54 30.41S 28.30E
Mount Gambier town 36 37.51S140.50E
Mount Goldsworthy town 32 20.20S119.31E
Mount Isa town 34 20.50S139.29E
Mount Magnet town 33 28.06S117.50E
Mountmellick 10 53.08N 7.21W
Mount Newman town 32 23.20S119.40E
Mount's B. 9 50.05N 5.25W
Mount Sturgeon town 34 20.08S144.00E
Mount Swan town 34 22.31S135.00E
Mount Vernon town 24 24.09S118.10E
Mount Willoughby 36 27.58S134.08E
Mourne Mts. 10 54.10N 6.02W
Moussoro 50 13.39N 16.29E
Moxico 52 11.50S 20.05E
Moy r. 10 54.10N 9.09W
Moyale 53 3.31N 39.04E
Moyowosi r. 53 4.59S 30.58E

ozambique 54 17.30S 35.45E
ozdok 21 43.45N 44.43E
ozyr 17 52.02N 29.10E
Pama r. 52 0.59S 15.40E
oanda 53 6.21S 31.01E
oika 53 11.52S 31.30E
porokoso 53 9.22S 30.06E
'Pouya 52 2.38S 16.08E
owapwa 53 6.23S 36.38E
sta r. 20 58.28N 31.20E
takuja 53 7.21S 30.37E
tsensk 20 53.18N 36.35E
twara 53 10.17S 40.11E
uang Chiang Rai 25 19.56N 99.51E
uang Nakhon Sawan 27 17.22N104.45E
ubende 53 0.30N 31.24E
uchinga Mts. 53 12.15S 31.00E
uck i. 11 56.50N 6.14W
ucojo 53 12.05S 40.26E
udanjiang 26 44.36N129.42E
ufulira 53 12.30S 28.12E
ugía 13 43.06N 9.14W
uğla 15 37.12N 28.22E
ühlhausen 16 51.12N 10.27E
uine Bheag town 10 52.42N 6.58W
uir, L. 33 34.30S116.30E
ukachevo 17 48.26N 22.45E
ukah 27 2.56N112.02E
ukawa 34 9.48S150.00E
ukinbudin 33 30.52S118.08E
ulanje Mts. 53 15.57S 35.33E
ulchén 49 37.43S 72.14W
ulgrave I. 34 10.07S142.08E
ulhacén mtn. 13 37.04N 3.22W
ulhouse 12 47.45N 7.21E
ull i. 11 56.28N 5.56W
ull, Sd. of str. 11 56.32N 5.55W
ullaghareirk Mts. 10 52.19N 9.06W
ullaghmore mtn. 10 54.51N 6.51W
ullaley 37 31.06S149.55E
ullet Pen. 10 54.12N 10.04W
ullingar 10 53.31N 7.21W
ull of Galloway c. 11 54.39N 4.52W
ull of Kintyre c. 11 55.17N 5.45W
ulobezi 54 16.49S 25.09E
ultān 25 30.11N 71.29E
ultyfarnham 10 53.37N 7.25W
umbwa 53 14.57S 27.01E
una i. 27 5.00S122.30E
ünchen 16 48.08N 11.35E
uncie 44 40.11N 85.23W
ungari 54 17.12S 33.31E
ungbere 53 2.40N 28.25E
unich see München 16
ünster N.-Westfalen 16 51.58N 7.37E
uonio 18 67.57N 23.42E
uonio r. 18 67.10N 23.40E
ur r. Austria see Mura r. 16
ura r. 16 46.18N 16.53E
uranga 53 0.43S 37.10E
urchison r. 32 27.30S114.10E
urcia 13 37.59N 1.08W
ureş r. 17 46.16N 20.10E
uret 12 43.28N 1.19E
urewa 54 17.40S 31.47E
urmansk 20 68.59N 33.08E
urom 20 55.04N 42.04E
uroran 26 42.21N140.59E
urray r.S.A. 36 35.23S139.20E
urray r.W.A. 33 32.35S115.46E
urray Bridge town 36 35.10S139.17E
urrumbidgee r. 36 34.38S143.10E
urrurundi 37 31.47S150.51E
urtoa 36 36.40S142.31E
urwāra 25 23.51N 80.24E
uş 21 38.45N 41.30E
uscat see Masqaţ 24
usgrave Ranges mts. 32 26.10S131.50E
ushie 52 2.59S 16.55E
usi r. 27 2.20S104.57E
uskegon 44 43.13N 86.15W
uskogee 41 35.45N 95.21W
usoma 53 1.31S 33.48E
usselburgh 11 55.57N 3.04W
ussende 52 10.33S 16.02E
ustjala 19 58.28N 22.14E
ut 21 36.38N 33.27E
utare 54 18.59S 32.40E
uyinga 53 2.48S 30.21E
uzaffarpur 25 26.07N 85.24E
vuma 54 19.16S 30.30E
wanza 52 7.51S 26.43E
waya Mbeya 53 9.33S 33.56E
weka 52 4.51S 21.34E
wene Ditu 52 7.04S 23.27E
wenezi r. 54 22.42S 31.45E
weru, L. 53 9.00S 28.40E
winilunga 52 11.44S 24.24E
yrdal 19 60.44N 7.08E
ysore 25 12.18N 76.37E
ytishchi 20 55.54N 37.47E
zimba 53 12.00S 33.39E

N

aas 10 53.13N 6.41W
acala 53 14.34S 40.41E
achingwea 53 10.21S 38.46E
aestved 19 55.14N 11.46E
āgāland d. 25 26.10N 94.30E
agano d. 28 35.33N137.50E
agasaki 26 32.45N129.52E
āgercoil 25 8.11N 77.30E
agles Mts. 10 52.06N 8.26W
agoya 28 35.10N136.55E
āgpur 25 21.09N 79.06E
agykanizsa 17 46.27N 17.01E
aha 26 26.10N127.40E
ain 39 56.30N 61.45W
airn 11 57.35N 3.52W
airobi 53 1.17S 36.50E
aivasha 53 0.44S 36.26E
akatsugawa 28 35.29N137.30E
akhodka 23 42.53N132.54E
akhon Ratchasima 27 14.58N102.06E
akskov 19 54.50N 11.09E
akuru 53 0.16S 36.04E
alchik 21 43.31N 43.38E
alón r. 13 43.35N 6.06W
amacurra 53 17.35S 37.00E
amanga 53 2.33S 36.48E
amangan 22 40.59N 71.41E
amapa 53 13.48S 39.44E
amaponda 53 15.51S 39.52E
amarroi 53 15.58S 36.55E
am Co l. 25 30.45N 90.30E
am Dinh 26 20.21N106.09E
amecala 53 12.50S 39.38E
Nametil 53 15.41S 39.30E
Namib Desert 54 23.00S 15.20E
Namibe 52 15.10S 12.10E
Namibia 54 21.30S 16.45E
Namlea 27 3.15S127.07E
Nampula 53 15.09S 39.14E
Namsos 18 64.28N 11.30E
Namur 16 50.28N 4.52E
Namutoni 54 18.48S 16.58E
Namwala 52 15.44S 26.25E
Nanaimo 38 49.08N123.58W
Nanchang 26 28.37N115.57E
Nancy 12 48.42N 6.12E
Nānder 25 19.09N 77.20E
Nandewar Range mts. 37 30.20S150.45E
Nānga Parbat mtn. 25 35.10N 74.35E
Nanjing 26 32.02N118.52E
Nan Ling mts. 26 25.10N110.00E
Nanning 26 22.48N108.10E
Nantes 12 47.14N 1.35W
Nantucket I. 44 41.16N 70.03W
Nantwich 8 53.05N 2.31W
Nanyang 26 33.07N112.30E
Nanyuki 53 0.01N 37.03E
Napier 29 39.29S176.58E
Naples see Napoli 14
Napoli 14 40.50N 14.14E
Napoli, Golfo di g. 14 40.42N 14.15E
Nara 28 34.41N135.50E
Naracoorte 36 36.58S140.46E
Nārāyanganj 25 23.37N 90.30E
Narbonne 12 43.11N 3.00E
Narembeen 33 32.04S118.23E
Nares Str. 39 78.30N 75.00W
Narmada r. 25 21.40N 73.00E
Narodnaya mtn. 20 65.00N 61.00E
Narok 53 1.04S 35.54E
Narrabri 37 30.20S149.49E
Narrandera 37 34.36S146.34E
Narran L. 37 29.40S147.25E
Narrogin 33 32.58S117.10E
Narva 20 59.22N 28.17E
Narvik 18 68.26N 17.25E
Nasarawa 50 8.35N 7.44E
Nashua N.H. 44 42.46N 71.27W
Nashville 41 36.10N 86.50W
Näsijärvi l. 19 61.37N 23.42E
Nāsik 25 19.59N 73.48E
Nāşir, Buḩayrat l. 24 22.40N 32.00E
Nassau 43 25.03N 77.20W
Nasser, L. see Nāşir, Buḩayrat l. 51
Nässjö 19 57.39N 14.41E
Natal 47 5.46S 35.15W
Natchez 41 31.22N 91.24W
Nauru 30 0.32S166.55E
Nava r. 53 1.45N 27.06E
Navalmoral de la Mata 13 39.54N 5.33W
Navan 10 53.39N 6.42W
Naver r. 11 58.32N 4.14W
Navlya 20 52.51N 34.30E
Navojoa 42 27.06N109.26W
Návpaktos 15 38.24N 21.49E
Návplion 15 37.33N 22.47E
Navrongo 50 10.51N 1.03W
Náxos i. 15 37.03N 25.30E
Nazas r. 42 25.34N103.25W
Nazilli 21 37.55N 28.20E
Ndalatando 52 9.12S 14.54E
N'Dendé 52 2.20S 11.23E
N'Djamena 50 12.10N 14.59E
Ndjolé 52 0.07S 10.45E
Ndola 53 12.58S 28.39E
Neagh, Lough 10 54.36N 6.25W
Neath 9 51.39N 3.49W
Nebit-Dag 21 39.31N 54.24E
Nebraska d. 40 41.30N100.00W
Neches r. 41 29.55N 93.50W
Neckar r. 16 49.32N 8.26E
Necochea 49 38.31S 58.46W
Necuto 52 4.55S 12.38E
Needles 40 34.51N114.36W
Nefyn 8 52.55N 4.31W
Negotin 17 44.14N 22.33E
Negrais, C. 25 16.00N 94.12E
Negro r. 49 40.50S 63.00W
Negro r. 46 3.00S 59.55W
Negro r. 49 33.27S 58.20W
Negros i. 27 10.00N123.00E
Neijiang 26 29.29N105.03E
Nei Monggol d. 26 41.00N112.00E
Neisse r. 16 52.05N 14.42E
Neiva 46 2.58N 75.15W
Neksö 19 55.04N 15.09E
Nellore 25 14.29N 80.00E
Nelson r. 39 57.00N 93.20W
Nelson d. 29 41.40S172.20E
Nelson 8 53.50N 2.14W
Nelson, C. 36 38.27S141.35E
Nelspruit 54 25.27S 30.58E
Néma 50 16.32N 7.12W
Neman r. 19 55.18N 21.23E
Nemours 12 48.16N 2.41E
Nenagh 10 52.52N 8.13W
Nenana 38 64.35N149.20W
Nene r. 8 52.49N 0.12E
Nepal 25 28.00N 84.00E
Nephin Beg Range mts. 10 54.00N 9.37W
Nera r. 14 42.33N 12.43E
Neretva r. 15 43.02N 17.28E
Neriquinha 52 15.50S 21.40E
Ness, Loch 11 57.16N 4.30W
Netherlands 16 52.00N 5.30E
Netherlands Antilles 43 12.30N 69.00W
Neto r. 15 39.12N 17.08E
Neubrandenburg 16 53.33N 13.16E
Neuchâtel 16 47.00N 6.56E
Neuchâtel, Lac de l. 16 46.55N 6.55E
Neufchâtel 12 49.44N 1.26E
Neuquén r. 49 39.02S 68.07W
Neuse r. 41 35.04N 77.04W
Neustrelitz 16 53.22N 13.05E
Neuwied 16 50.26N 7.28E
Nevada d. 40 39.00N117.00W
Nevada, Sierra mts. Spain 13 37.04N 3.20W
Nevada, Sierra mts. U.S.A. 40 37.30N119.00W
Nevel 20 56.00N 29.59E
Nevers 12 47.00N 3.09E
Nevertire 37 31.52S147.47E
Nevşehir 21 38.38N 34.43E
New Amsterdam 47 6.18N 57.30W
Newark N.J. 44 40.44N 74.11W
Newark-on-Trent 8 53.06N 0.48E
New Bedford 44 41.38N 70.56W
New Bern 41 35.05N 77.04W
Newbiggin-by-the-Sea 8 55.11N 1.30W
New Brunswick d. 44 46.30N 66.15W
New Brunswick 44 40.29N 74.27W
Newburgh 44 41.30N 74.00W
Newbury 9 51.24N 1.19W
New Caledonia is. see Nouvelle Calédonie is. 30
Newcastle Australia 37 32.55S151.46E
Newcastle U.K. 10 54.13N 5.53W
Newcastle Emlyn 9 52.02N 4.29W
Newcastle-under-Lyme 8 53.02N 2.15W
Newcastle upon Tyne 8 54.58N 1.36W
Newcastle West 10 52.26N 9.04W
New Delhi 25 28.36N 77.12E
New England Range mts. 37 30.30S151.50E
Newent 9 51.56N 2.24W
New Forest f. 9 50.50N 1.35W
Newfoundland d. 39 55.00N 60.00W
Newfoundland i. 39 48.30N 56.00W
New Galloway 11 55.05N 4.09W
New Guinea i. 27 5.00S140.00E
New Hampshire d. 44 43.35N 71.40W
Newhaven 9 50.47N 0.04E
New Haven 44 41.18N 72.55W
New Jersey d. 44 40.15N 74.30W
New London Conn. 44 41.21N 72.06W
Newmarket 9 52.15N 0.23E
Newmarket on Fergus 10 52.46N 8.55W
New Mexico d. 40 34.00N106.00W
New Norfolk 35 42.46S147.02E
New Orleans 41 30.00N 90.03W
New Plymouth 29 39.03S174.04E
Newport Mayo 10 53.53N 9.34W
Newport Tipperary 10 52.42N 8.25W
Newport Dyfed 9 52.01N 4.51W
Newport Essex 9 51.58N 0.13E
Newport Gwent 9 51.34N 2.59W
Newport Hants. 9 50.43N 1.18W
Newport R.I. 44 41.13N 71.18W
Newquay 9 50.24N 5.06W
New Quay 9 52.13N 4.22W
New Radnor 9 52.15N 3.10W
New Romney 9 50.59N 0.58E
New Ross 10 52.24N 6.57W
Newry 10 54.11N 6.21W
New Scone 11 56.25N 3.25W
New South Wales d. 37 32.40S147.40E
Newton Abbot 9 50.32N 3.37W
Newton Aycliffe 8 54.36N 1.34W
Newtonmore 11 57.04N 4.08W
Newton Stewart 11 54.57N 4.29W
Newtown 9 52.31N 3.19W
Newtownabbey 10 54.39N 5.57W
Newtownards 10 54.35N 5.41W
Newtown Butler 10 54.12N 7.22W
Newtown St. Boswells 11 55.35N 2.40W
Newtownstewart 10 54.43N 7.25W
New York 44 40.40N 73.50W
New York d. 44 43.00N 75.00W
New Zealand 29 41.00S175.00E
Nezhin 17 51.03N 31.54E
Ngami, L. 54 20.32S 22.38E
Ngamiland f. 54 20.00S 22.30E
N'Gao 52 2.28S 15.40E
Ngaoundéré 50 7.20N 13.35E
Ngaruawahia 29 37.40S175.09E
Ngaruroro r. 29 39.34S176.54E
N'Giva 52 17.03S 15.47E
Ngong 53 1.22S 36.40E
Ngonye Falls f. 52 16.35S 23.39E
Ngozi 53 2.52S 29.50E
Nguigmi 50 14.00N 13.06E
Nha Trang 27 12.15N109.10E
Nhill 36 36.20S141.40E
Niagara Falls town 44 43.06N 79.02W
Niamey 50 13.32N 2.05E
Niangara 53 3.47N 27.54E
Niassa d. 53 13.00S 36.30E
Nicaragua 43 13.00N 85.00W
Nicaragua, Lago de l. 43 11.30N 85.30W
Nicastro 14 38.58N 16.16E
Nice 12 43.42N 7.16E
Nicobar Islands 25 8.00N 93.30E
Nicosia see Levkosía 24
Nicoya, Golfo de g. 43 9.30N 85.00W
Nid r. 19 58.24N 8.48E
Niğde 21 37.58N 34.42E
Niger 50 17.00N 9.30E
Niger r. 50 4.15N 6.05E
Nigeria 50 9.00N 7.30E
Niigata 26 37.58N139.02E
Niiza 28 35.48N139.34E
Nijmegen 16 51.50N 5.52E
Nikel 18 69.20N 30.00E
Nikiniki 27 9.49S124.29E
Nikki 50 9.55N 3.18E
Nikolayev 21 46.57N 32.00E
Nikolayevsk-na-Amure 23 53.20N140.44E
Nikopol 21 47.34N 34.25E
Niksar 21 40.35N 36.59E
Nīl, An r. 51 31.30N 30.25E
Nile r. see Nīl, An r. 51
Niles Mich. 44 41.51N 86.15W
Nilgiri Hills 25 11.30N 77.30E
Nîmes 12 43.50N 4.21E
Ningbo 26 29.56N121.32E
Niobrara r. 40 42.45N 98.10W
Nioro 50 15.12N 9.35W
Niort 12 46.19N 0.27W
Nipigon, L. 44 49.50N 88.30W
Nipissing, L. 44 46.17N 80.00W
Niš 15 43.20N 21.54E
Niterói 45 22.54S 43.06W
Nith r. 11 55.00N 3.35W
Niue i. 30 19.02S169.52W
Nizāmābād 25 18.40N 78.05E
Nizhneudinsk 23 54.55N 99.00E
Nizhnevartovsk 22 60.57N 76.40E
Nizhniy Tagil 20 58.00N 60.00E
Njombe r. 53 7.02S 35.55E
Njoro 53 5.16S 36.30E
Nkhata Bay town 53 11.37S 34.20E
Nkhotakota 53 12.55S 34.19E
Nkungwe Mt. 53 6.15S 29.54E
Noatak 38 67.34N162.59W
Nogales 42 31.20N111.00W
Nogent-le-Rotrou 12 48.19N 0.50E
Noguera Ribagorçana r. 13 41.27N 0.25E
Noirmoutier, Île de i. 12 47.00N 2.15W
Nokia 19 61.28N 23.30E
Nola 52 3.28N 16.08E
Noma Omuramba r. 54 19.14S 22.15E
Nome 38 64.30N165.30W
Noorvik 38 66.50N161.14W
Nordenham 16 53.30N 8.29E
Nordfriesische Inseln is. 16 54.30N 8.00E
Nordvik 23 73.40N110.50E
Nore r. 10 52.25N 6.58W
Norfolk d. 9 52.39N 1.00E
Norfolk Va. 41 36.54N 76.18W
Norfolk Broads f. 8 52.43N 1.35E
Norilsk 23 69.21N 88.02E
Normanton 34 17.40S141.05E
Norman Wells 38 65.19N126.46W
Nörresundby 19 57.04N 9.56E
Norris L. 41 36.20N 83.55W
Norristown 44 40.07N 75.20W
Norrköping 19 58.36N 16.11E
Norrtälje 19 59.46N 18.42E
Norseman 33 32.15S121.47E
Norte, C. 47 1.40N 49.55W
Northallerton 8 54.20N 1.26W
Northam 33 31.41S116.40E
Northampton 9 52.14N 0.54W
Northamptonshire d. 9 52.18N 0.55W
North Battleford 38 52.47N108.19W
North Bay town 44 46.19N 79.28W
North Bend Oreg. 40 43.26N124.14W
North Berwick 11 56.04N 2.43W
North C. 29 34.28S173.00E
North Canadian r. 41 35.30N 95.45W
North Carolina d. 41 35.30N 79.00W
North Channel 10 55.15N 5.52W
North China Plain f. see Huabei Pingyuan f. 26
North Dakota d. 40 47.00N100.00W
North Downs hills 9 51.18N 0.40E
Northern Ireland d. 10 54.40N 6.45W
Northern Territory d. 34 20.00S133.00E
North Esk r. 11 56.45N 2.25W
North Foreland c. 9 51.23N 1.26E
North Frisian Is. see Nordfriesische Inseln is. 16
North I. 29 39.00S175.00E
Northiam 9 50.59N 0.39E
North Korea 26 40.00N128.00E
Northland d. 29 35.25S174.00E
North Platte r. 40 41.09N100.55W
North Ronaldsay i. 11 59.23N 2.26W
North Sea 7 56.00N 5.00E
North Sporades see Voríai Sporádhes is. 15
North Taranaki Bight b. 29 38.45S174.15E
North Tawton 9 50.48N 3.55W
North Uist i. 11 57.35N 7.20W
Northumberland d. 8 55.12N 2.00W
North Walsham 8 52.49N 1.22E
Northway 38 62.58N142.00W
North West Highlands 11 57.30N 5.15W
North West River town 39 53.30N 60.10W
Northwest Territories d. 39 66.00N 95.00W
Northwich 8 53.16N 2.30W
North York Moors hills 8 54.21N 0.50W
North Yorkshire d. 8 54.14N 1.14W
Norton Sound b. 38 63.50N164.00W
Norwalk Conn. 44 41.07N 73.25W
Norway 18 65.00N 13.00E
Norway House town 39 53.59N 97.50W
Norwich 9 52.38N 1.17E
Noss Head 11 58.28N 3.03W
Noteć r. 16 52.44N 15.26E
Nottingham 8 52.57N 1.10W
Nottinghamshire d. 8 53.10N 1.00W
Nouadhibou 50 20.54N 17.01W
Nouakchott 50 18.09N 15.58W
Nouméa 30 22.16S166.27E
Nouvelle Anvers 52 1.38N 19.10E
Nouvelle Calédonie is. 30 21.30S165.30E
Nova Gaia 52 10.09S 17.35E
Nova Iguaçu 45 22.45S 43.27W
Novara 14 45.27N 8.37E
Nova Scotia d. 39 45.00N 64.00W
Nova Sofala 54 20.09S 34.24E
Novaya Ladoga 20 60.09N 32.15E
Novelda 13 38.24N 0.45W
Novgorod 20 58.30N 31.20E
Novi Pazar 15 43.08N 20.28E
Novi Sad 17 45.16N 19.52E
Novocherkassk 21 47.25N 40.05E
Novograd Volynskiy 17 50.34N 27.32E
Novogrudok 17 53.35N 25.50E
Novo Hamburgo 45 29.37S 51.07W
Novokazalinsk 22 45.48N 62.06E
Novokuznetsk 22 53.45N 87.12E
Novomoskovsk R.S.F.S.R. 20 54.06N 38.15E
Novorossiysk 21 44.44N 37.46E
Novoshakhtinsk 21 47.46N 39.55E
Novosibirsk 22 55.04N 82.55E
Novouzensk 21 50.29N 48.08E
Novyy Port 22 67.38N 72.33E
Nowa Ruda 16 50.34N 16.30E
Nowa Sól 16 51.49N 15.41E
Nowra 37 35.54S150.36E
Nowy Sącz 17 49.39N 20.40E
Noyon 12 49.35N 3.00E
Nsanje 53 16.55S 35.12E
Nubian Desert 51 21.00N 34.00E
Nueces r. 41 27.55N 97.30W
Nueva Gerona 43 21.53N 82.49W
Nuevitas 43 21.34N 77.18W
Nuevo Laredo 42 27.30N 99.30W
Nu Jiang r. China see Salween r. 26
Nuku'alofa 31 21.07S175.12W
Nullarbor Plain f. 33 31.30S128.00E
Numazu 28 35.06N138.52E
Nuneaton 9 52.32N 1.29W
Nungo 53 13.25S 37.45E
Nunivak I. 38 60.00N166.30W
Nürnberg 16 49.27N 11.05E
Nusaybin 21 37.05N 41.11E
Nuweveldberge mts. 54 32.15S 21.50E
Nyahururu Falls town 53 0.04N 36.22E
Nyakanazi 53 3.05S 31.16E
Nyala 51 12.01N 24.50E
Nyamandhlovu 54 19.50S 28.15E
Nyanga r. 52 3.00S 10.17E
Nyanza 53 2.20S 29.42E
Nyborg 19 55.19N 10.48E
Nybro 19 56.45N 15.54E
Nyeri 53 0.22S 36.56E
Nyika Plateau f. 53 10.25S 33.50E
Nyköping 19 58.45N 17.00E
Nylstroom 54 24.42S 28.24E
Nynäshamn 19 58.54N 17.57E
Nyong r. 52 3.15N 9.55E
Nyons 12 44.22N 5.08E
Nyunzu 53 5.55S 28.00E
Nzega 53 4.13S 33.09E
Nzeto 52 7.13S 12.56E

O

Oahe Resr. 40 45.45N100.20W
Oakland Calif. 40 37.50N122.15W
Oakville 44 43.27N 79.41W
Oamaru 29 45.07S170.58E
Oaxaca 42 17.05N 96.41W
Ob r. 20 66.50N 69.00E
Oba 44 49.04N 84.07W
Oban 11 56.26N 5.28W
Obbia 51 5.20N 48.30E
Oberá 48 27.30S 55.07W
Obi i. 27 1.45S127.30E
Ocaña 46 8.16N 73.21W
Ocean I. see Banaba i. 30 0.52S169.35E
Ochil Hills 11 56.16N 3.25W
Ocotal 43 13.37N 86.31W
Ocotlán 42 20.21N102.42W
Ocua 53 13.40S 39.46E
Oda 50 5.55N 0.56W
Odawara 28 35.15N139.10E
Odda 19 60.04N 6.33E
Ödemiş 15 38.12N 28.00E
Odense 19 55.24N 10.23E
Odenwald mts. 16 49.40N 9.20E
Oder r. E. Germany see Odra r. 16
Odessa 24 46.30N 30.46E
Odorhei 17 46.18N 25.18E
Ofanto r. 14 41.22N 16.12E
Offaly d. 10 53.15N 7.30W
Offenbach 16 50.06N 8.46E
Offenburg 16 48.29N 7.57E
Ōgaki 28 35.21N136.37E
Ogbomosho 50 8.05N 4.11E
Ogden Utah 40 41.14N111.59W
Ogeechee r. 41 32.54N 81.05W
Ognon r. 12 47.20N 5.37E
Ogoja 50 6.40N 8.45E
Ogooué r. 52 1.00S 9.05E
Ogosta r. 15 43.44N 23.51E
Ogulin 16 45.17N 15.14E
Ohio d. 44 40.15N 82.45W
Ohio r. 44 36.59N 89.08W
Ohře r. 16 50.32N 14.08E
Ohrid 15 41.06N 20.48E
Oise r. 12 49.00N 2.10E
Ojocaliente 42 22.35N102.18W
Ojo de Agua 48 29.30S 63.44W
Oka r. 20 56.09N 43.00E
Okahandja 54 21.58S 16.44E
Okanogan r. 40 47.45N120.05W
Okavango r. 54 18.30S 22.04E
Okavango Basin f. 54 19.30S 22.30E
Okazaki 28 34.57N137.10E
Okeechobee, L. 41 27.00N 80.45W
Okefenokee Swamp f. 41 30.40N 82.40W
Okehampton 9 50.44N 4.01W
Okere r. 53 1.37N 33.53E
Okha 23 53.35N142.50E
Okhotsk 23 59.20N143.15E
Okhotsk, Sea of 23 55.00N150.00E
Okinawa jima i. 26 26.30N128.00E
Okipoko r. 54 18.40S 16.03E
Oklahoma d. 41 35.00N 97.00W
Oklahoma City 41 35.28N 97.33W
Öland i. 19 56.45N 16.38E
Olary 36 32.18S140.19E
Olavarría 49 36.57S 60.20W
Oldenburg Nschn. 16 53.08N 8.13E
Oldham 8 53.33N 2.08W
Old Head of Kinsale c. 10 51.37N 8.33W
Olenëk r. 23 73.00N120.00E
Oléron, Île d' i. 12 45.55N 1.16W
Olga 23 43.46N135.14E
Olhão 13 37.01N 7.50W
Olifants r. C.P. 54 31.42S 18.10E
Olifants r. Trans. 54 24.08S 32.39E
Ólimbos 15 35.44N 27.11E
Ólimbos mtn. 15 40.04N 22.20E
Oliva 48 32.05S 63.35W
Olivares 13 39.45N 2.21W
Olney 9 52.09N 0.42W
Olomouc 17 49.36N 17.16E
Oloron 12 43.12N 0.35W
Olot 13 42.11N 2.30E
Olsztynek 17 53.36N 20.17E
Olteţ r. 17 44.13N 24.28E
Olympus mtn. see Ólimbos mtn. 15
Omagh 10 54.36N 7.20W
Omaha 41 41.15N 96.00W
Oman 24 22.30N 57.30E
Oman, G. of 24 25.00N 58.00E
Omaruru 54 21.25S 15.57E
Omdurman see Umm Durmān 51
Omolon r. 23 68.50N158.30E
Omsk 22 55.00N 73.22E
Omulew r. 17 53.05N 21.32E
Oña 13 42.44N 3.25W
Onega r. 20 63.59N 38.11E
Onitsha 50 6.10N 6.47E
Onslow 32 21.41S115.12E
Ontario d. 39 52.00N 86.00W
Ontario Oreg. 40 44.02N116.58W
Ontario, L. 44 43.45N 78.00W
Oostende 16 51.13N 2.55E
Opole 17 50.40N 17.56E
Oporto see Porto 13
Opotiki 29 38.00S177.18E
Oradea 17 47.03N 21.55E
Oran 50 35.45N 0.38W
Orange 12 44.08N 4.48E
Orange r. 54 28.38S 16.38E
Orangeburg 41 33.28N 80.53W
Oranjemund 54 28.35S 16.26E
Orbost 37 37.42S148.30E
Orchila i. 43 11.52N 66.10W
Ord r. 32 15.30S128.30E
Ordu 21 41.00N 37.52E
Orduña 13 43.00N 3.00W
Ordzhonikidze 21 43.02N 44.43E
Örebro 19 59.17N 15.13E
Oregon d. 40 44.00N120.00W
Öregrund 19 60.20N 18.26E
Orekhovo-Zuyevo 20 55.47N 39.00E
Orel 20 52.58N 36.04E
Orenburg 20 51.50N 55.00E
Orense 13 42.20N 7.52W
Orihuela 13 38.05N 0.56W
Orinoco r. 46 9.00N 61.30W
Orissa d. 25 20.20N 84.00E
Oristano 14 39.53N 8.36E
Orizaba 42 18.51N 97.08W
Orkney Is. d. 11 59.00N 3.00W
Orlando 41 28.33N 81.21W
Orléans 12 47.54N 1.54E
Ormond 29 38.35S177.58E
Ormskirk 8 53.35N 2.53W
Orne r. 12 49.17N 0.10W
Örnsköldsvik 18 63.17N 18.50E
Oromocto 44 45.50N 66.28W
Orosei 14 40.23N 9.40E
Oroville Wash. 40 48.57N119.27W
Orsha 20 54.30N 30.23E
Orsk 20 51.13N 58.35E
Orşova 17 44.42N 22.22E
Orthez 12 43.29N 0.46W
Oryakhovo 15 43.42N 23.58E
Ōsaka 28 34.40N135.30E
Osh 22 40.37N 72.49E
Oshawa 44 43.54N 78.51W
Ō shima i. Tosan 28 34.43N139.24E
Oshogbo 50 7.50N 4.35E
Oshwe 52 3.27S 19.32E
Osijek 15 45.35N 18.43E
Oskarshamn 19 57.16N 16.26E
Oskol r. 21 49.08N 37.10E
Oslo 19 59.56N 10.45E
Osmancik 21 40.58N 34.50E
Osmaniye 21 37.04N 36.15E
Osnabrück 16 52.17N 8.03E
Osorno 49 40.35S 73.14W
Ossa, Mt. 35 41.52S146.04E
Ostashkov 20 57.09N 33.10E
Ostend see Oostende 16
Österdal r. 19 61.03N 14.30E
Österö i. 18 62.10N 7.00W
Östersund 18 63.10N 14.40E
Ostrava 17 49.50N 18.15E
Ostrov 20 57.22N 28.22E
Ostrów Mazowiecka 17 52.50N 21.51E
Osuna 13 37.14N 5.06W
Oswestry 8 52.52N 3.03W
Otago d. 29 45.10S169.20E
Otago Pen. 29 45.48S170.45E
Otavi 54 19.37S 17.21E
Otju 54 18.15S 13.18E
Otra r. 19 58.09N 8.00E
Otranto 15 40.09N 18.30E
Otranto, Str. of 15 40.10N 19.00E
Otta 19 61.46N 9.32E
Ottawa 44 45.25N 75.43W
Ottawa r. 44 45.20N 73.58W
Ottawa Is. 39 59.50N 80.00W
Otter r. 9 50.38N 3.19W
Otterburn 8 55.14N 2.10W
Ottumwa 41 41.02N 92.26W
Otway, C. 36 38.51S143.34E
Ouachita r. 41 33.10N 92.10W
Ouachita Mts. 41 34.40N 94.30W
Ouagadougou 50 12.20N 1.40W
Ouahigouya 50 13.31N 2.21W
Ouargla 50 32.00N 5.16E
Oudtshoorn 54 33.35S 22.11E
Ouessant, Île d' i. 12 48.28N 5.05W
Ouesso 52 1.38N 16.03E
Oughter, Lough 10 54.01N 7.28W
Oujda 50 34.41N 1.45W
Oulu 18 65.01N 25.28E
Oulu r. 18 65.01N 25.25E
Oulujärvi l. 18 64.20N 27.15E
Oundle 9 52.28N 0.28W
Ourinhos 45 23.00S 49.54W
Ouse r. Humber. 8 53.41N 0.42W
Outer Hebrides is. 11 57.40N 7.35W
Outjo 54 20.07S 16.10E
Ouyen 36 35.06S142.22E
Ovamboland f. 54 17.45S 16.00E
Oviedo 13 43.21N 5.50W
Owando 52 0.30S 15.48E
Owen Falls Dam 53 0.30N 33.07E
Owen Stanley Range mts. 34 9.30S148.00E
Oxelösund 19 58.40N 17.06E
Oxford 9 51.45N 1.15W
Oxfordshire d. 9 51.46N 1.10W
Oxley 36 34.11S144.10E
Oykel r. 11 57.53N 4.21W
Oymyakon 23 63.30N142.44E
Ozark Plateau 41 36.00N 93.35W

P

Paarl 54 33.44S 18.58E
Pachuca 42 20.10N 98.44W
Pacific Ocean 31
Padang 27 0.55S100.21E
Paderborn 16 51.43N 8.44E
Padova 14 45.27N 11.52E
Padre I. 41 27.00N 97.20W
Padstow 9 50.33N 4.57W
Padua see Padova 16
Paeroa 29 37.23S175.41E
Paible 11 57.35N 7.27W
Paihia 29 35.16S174.05E
Päijänne l. 19 61.35N 25.30E
Paisley 11 55.50N 4.26W
Pakanbaru 27 0.33N101.20E
Pakistan 25 31.00N 70.00E
Pakwach 53 2.27N 31.18E
Palana 23 59.05N159.59E
Palapye 54 22.33S 27.07E
Palawan i. 27 9.30N118.30E
Paldiski 19 59.20N 24.06E
Palembang 27 2.59S104.50E
Palencia 13 42.01N 4.34W
Palermo 14 38.09N 13.22E
Palliser, C. 29 41.35S175.15E
Palma 13 39.36N 2.39E
Palma, Bahía de b. 13 39.30N 2.40E
Palma del Río 13 37.43N 5.17W
Palmas, Golfo di g. 14 39.00N 8.30E
Palmerston North 29 40.20S175.39E
Palmi 14 38.22N 15.50E
Palmira 46 3.33N 76.17W
Palm Springs town 40 33.49N116.34W
Palmyras Pt. 25 20.46N 87.02E
Pamiers 12 43.07N 1.36E
Pamir mts. 22 38.00N 73.30E
Pampa 40 35.32N100.58W
Pampas f. 49 34.00S 64.00W
Pamplona 13 42.49N 1.39W
Panama 43 9.00N 80.00W
Panamá town 43 8.57N 79.30W
Panamá, Golfo de g. 43 8.30N 79.00W
Panama City 41 30.10N 85.41W
Panay i. 27 11.10N122.30E
Panevežys 19 55.44N 24.21E
Pangi 52 3.10S 26.38E
Pangnirtung 39 66.05N 65.45W
Pantano del Esla l. 13 41.40N 5.50W
Pantelleria i. 14 36.48N 12.00E
Paola 14 39.21N 16.03E
Papeete 31 17.32S149.34W
Papenburg 16 53.03N 7.23E
Paracatu r. 45 16.30S 45.10W
Paraguaçu r. 47 12.35S 38.59W
Paraguarí 45 25.36S 57.06W
Paraguay r. 45 27.30S 58.50W
Paraguay 45 23.00S 57.00W
Paraíba r. 45 21.45S 41.10W
Parakou 50 9.23N 2.40E
Paramaribo 47 5.52N 55.14W
Paraná 49 31.45S 60.30W
Paraná r. 49 34.00S 58.30W
Paranã r. 47 12.30S 48.10W
Paranaguá 45 25.32S 48.36W
Paranaíba r. 45 20.00S 51.00W
Paranapanema r. 45 22.30S 53.03W
Paranapiacaba, Serra mts. 45 24.30S 49.15W
Paranavaí 45 23.02S 52.36W
Paraparaumu 29 40.55S175.00E
Pardo r. Bahia 45 15.40S 39.38W
Pardo r. Mato Grosso 45 21.56S 52.07W
Pardo r. São Paulo 45 20.10S 48.36W
Pardubice 16 50.03N 15.45E
Paris 12 48.52N 2.20E
Parkano 19 62.01N 23.01E
Parker Dam 40 34.25N114.05W
Parkersburg 44 39.17N 81.33W
Parkes 37 33.10S148.13E
Parma 14 44.48N 10.18E
Parnaíba r. 47 2.58S 41.47W
Parnassós mtn. 15 38.33N 22.35E
Pärnu r. 19 58.23N 24.29E
Paroo r. 36 31.30S143.34E
Páros i. 15 37.04N 25.11E
Parral 49 36.09S 71.50W
Parramatta 37 33.50S150.57E
Parry Is. 39 76.00N102.00W
Parseta r. 16 54.12N 15.33E
Parthenay 12 46.39N 0.14W
Partry Mts. 10 53.40N 9.30W
Parys 54 26.54S 27.26E
Pasadena Calif. 40 34.10N118.09W
Pascua, Isla de i. 31 27.08S109.23W
Passau 16 48.35N 13.28E
Passo Fundo 45 28.16S 52.20W
Passos 45 20.45S 46.38W
Patagonia f. 49 42.20S 67.00W
Pate I. 53 2.08S 41.02E
Paterson 44 40.55N 74.10W
Pathfinder Resr. 40 42.25N106.55W
Patía r. 46 1.54N 78.30W
Patkai Hills 25 26.30N 95.30E
Pátmos i. 15 37.20N 26.33E
Patna 25 25.36N 85.07E
Patos de Minas 45 18.35S 46.32W
Pátrai 15 38.15N 21.45E
Patraïkós Kólpos g. 15 38.15N 21.35E
Patrickswell 10 52.36N 8.43W
Patuca r. 43 15.50N 84.18W
Pau 12 43.18N 0.22W
Pauillac 12 45.12N 0.44W
Pavia 14 45.10N 9.10E
Pavlodar 22 52.21N 76.59E
Paysandú 49 32.19S 58.05W
Peace r. 38 59.00N111.26W
Peace River town 38 56.15N117.18W
Peak Hill town N.S.W. 37 32.47S148.13E
Pearl r. 41 30.15N 89.25W
Pebane 53 17.14S 38.10E
Peć 15 42.40N 20.17E
Pechenga 18 69.28N 31.04E
Pechora r. 20 68.10N 54.00E
Pechorskoye More sea 20 69.00N 55.00E
Pecos r. 40 29.45N101.25W
Pécs 17 46.05N 18.14E
Pedro Juan Caballero 45 22.30S 55.44W
Peebinga 36 34.55S140.57E
Peebles 11 55.39N 3.12W
Peel r. 38 68.13N135.00W
Peel 8 54.14N 4.42W
Peene r. 16 53.53N 13.49E
Pegasus B. 29 43.15S173.00E
Pegu 27 17.20N 96.36E
Pehuajó 49 35.50S 61.50W
Peking see Beijing 26
Peleng i. 27 1.30S123.10E
Pelly r. 38 62.50N137.35W
Pelotas 45 31.45S 52.20W
Pematangsiantar 27 2.59N 99.01E
Pemba I. 53 5.10S 39.45E
Pembroke 9 51.41N 4.57W
Peñaranda de Bracamonte 13 40.54N 5.13W
Penarth 9 51.26N 3.11W
Peñas, Cabo de c. 13 43.42N 5.52W
Pendine 9 51.44N 4.33W
Penge 52 5.31S 24.37E
Penicuik 11 55.49N 3.13W
Pennsylvania d. 44 40.45N 77.30W
Penny Highland mtn. 39 67.10N 66.50W
Penola 36 37.23S140.21E
Penonomé 43 8.30N 80.20W
Penrith 8 54.40N 2.45W
Penryn 9 50.10N 5.07W
Pensacola 41 30.30N 87.12W
Penticton 38 49.29N119.38W
Pentland Firth str. 11 58.40N 3.00W
Pentland Hills 11 55.50N 3.20W
Penzance 9 50.07N 5.32W
Pereira 46 4.47N 75.46W
Pergamino 49 33.53S 60.35W
Péribonca r. 44 48.45N 72.05W
Périgueux 12 45.12N 0.44E
Perm 20 58.01N 56.10E
Péronne 12 49.56N 2.57E
Perpignan 12 42.42N 2.54E
Perranporth 9 50.21N 5.09W
Perth Australia 33 31.58S115.49E
Perth U.K. 11 56.24N 3.28W
Peru 46 10.00S 75.00W
Perugia 14 43.06N 12.24E
Pervouralsk 20 56.59N 59.58E
Pesaro 14 43.54N 12.54E
Pescara 14 42.27N 14.13E
Pescara r. 14 42.28N 14.13E
Peshāwar 25 34.01N 71.33E
Petatlán 42 17.31N101.16W
Petauke 53 14.16S 31.21E
Peterborough 9 52.35N 0.14W
Peterhead 11 57.30N 1.46W
Peterlee 8 54.45N 1.18W
Petersfield 9 51.00N 0.56W
Petropavlovsk 22 54.53N 69.13E
Petropavlovsk Kamchatskiy 23 53.03N158.43E
Petrópolis 45 22.30S 43.06W
Petrovsk 20 52.20N 45.24E

Petrovsk Zabaykal'skiy 23 51.20N108.55E
Petrozavodsk 20 61.46N 34.19E
Pforzheim 16 48.53N 8.41E
Phangnga 27 8.29N 98.31E
Philadelphia Penn. 44 39.57N 75.07W
Philippines 27 13.00N123.00E
Philippine Sea 30 18.00N 135.00E
Philipstown 54 30.25S 24.26E
Phnum Pénh 27 11.35N104.55E
Phoenix Ariz. 40 33.30N111.55W
Phoenix Is. 30 4.00S 172.00W
Phuket 27 7.55N 98.23E
Piacenza 14 45.03N 9.42E
Piangil 36 35.04S143.20E
Pianosa i. 14 42.35N 10.05E
Piave r. 14 45.33N 12.45E
Pic r. 44 48.36N 86.28W
Picardie d. 12 49.42N 2.40E
Pickering 8 54.15N 0.46W
Pickwick L. resr. 41 35.00N 88.10W
Picton 37 34.12S150.35E
Picton 29 41.17S174.02E
Piedras Negras 42 28.40N100.32W
Pierre 40 44.23N100.20W
Pietermaritzburg 54 29.36S 30.23E
Pietersburg 54 23.54S 29.27E
Piet Retief 54 27.00S 30.49E
Pikes Peak mtn. 40 38.50N105.03W
Piketberg 54 32.54S 18.43E
Piła 16 53.09N 16.44E
Pilcomayo r. 48 25.15S 57.43W
Pílos 15 36.55N 21.40E
Pinang, Pulau i. 27 5.30N100.10E
Pinarbaşi 21 38.43N 36.23E
Píndhos Óros mts. 15 39.40N 21.00E
Pine Bluff town 41 34.13N 92.00W
Ping r. 27 15.47N100.05E
Pingliang 26 35.21N107.12E
Piniós r. 15 39.51N 22.37E
Pinnaroo 36 35.18S140.54E
Pinsk 17 52.08N 26.01E
Pinto 48 29.09S 62.38W
Piombino 14 42.56N 10.30E
Piracicaba 45 22.45S 47.40W
Piraeus see Piraiévs 15
Piraiévs 15 37.56N 23.38E
Pirna 16 50.58N 13.58E
Pirot 15 43.10N 22.32E
Pisa 14 43.43N 10.24E
Pisciotta 14 40.08N 15.12E
Písek 16 49.19N 14.10E
Pita 50 11.05N 12.15W
Pitcairn I. 31 25.04S130.06W
Piteå 16 65.20N 21.30E
Piteşti 17 44.52N 24.51E
Pitlochry 11 56.43N 3.45W
Pittsburgh 44 40.26N 80.00W
Pittsfield 44 42.27N 73.15W
Piura 46 5.15S 80.38W
Plasencia 13 40.02N 6.05W
Platani r. 14 37.24N 13.15E
Plate, R. est. see La Plata, Río de 49
Platinum 38 59.00N161.50W
Platte r. 41 41.05N 96.50W
Plauen 16 50.29N 12.08E
Pleiku 27 13.57N108.01E
Plenty, B. of 29 37.40S176.50E
Pleven 15 43.25N 24.39E
Ploieşti 17 44.57N 26.02E
Plombières 12 47.58N 6.28E
Plovdiv 15 42.09N 24.45E
Plumtree 54 20.30S 27.50E
Plymouth 9 50.23N 4.09W
Plzeň 16 49.45N 13.22E
Po r. 14 44.51N 12.30E
Pobla de Segur 13 42.15N 0.58E
Pocatello 40 42.53N112.26W
Pocklington 8 53.56N 0.48W
Poços de Caldas 45 21.48S 46.33W
Podolsk 20 55.23N 37.32E
Podor 50 16.40N 14.57W
Pofadder 54 29.08S 19.22E
Poh 27 1.00S122.50E
Pointe-à-Pitre 43 16.14N 61.32W
Pointe Noire town 52 4.46S 11.53E
Poitiers 12 46.35N 0.20E
Pokhara 25 28.12N 83.59E
Poko 52 3.08N 26.51E
Poland 17 52.30N 19.00E
Polatlı 21 39.34N 32.08E
Poligny 12 46.50N 5.42E
Pollino mtn. 14 39.53N 16.11E
Polperro 9 50.19N 4.31W
Poltava 21 49.35N 34.35E
Polynesia is. 30 4.00S165.00W
Pombal 47 6.45S 37.45W
Ponce 43 18.00N 66.40W
Ponferrada 13 42.32N 6.31W
Pongola r. 54 26.13S 32.38E
Ponta Grossa 45 25.00S 50.09W
Ponta Porã 45 22.27S 55.39W
Pontefract 8 53.42N 1.19W
Pontevedra 13 42.25N 8.39W
Pontiac Mich. 44 42.39N 83.18W
Pontianak 27 0.05S109.16E
Pontoise 12 49.03N 2.05E
Pontrilas 9 51.56N 2.53W
Pontypool 9 51.42N 3.01W
Pontypridd 9 51.36N 3.21W
Poole 9 50.42N 2.02W
Poplar Bluff town 41 36.40N 90.25W
Popocatépetl mtn. 42 19.02N 98.38W
Popokabaka 52 5.41S 16.40E
Popondetta 34 8.45S148.15E
Porbandar 25 21.38N 69.36E
Porcupine r. 38 66.25N145.20W
Pori 19 61.29N 21.47E
Porirua 29 41.08S174.50E
Porkkala 19 59.59N 24.26E
Pornic 12 47.07N 2.05W
Poronaysk 23 49.13N142.55E
Porsgrunn 19 59.09N 9.40E
Port Adelaide 36 34.52S138.30E
Portadown 10 54.25N 6.27W
Portaferry 10 54.23N 5.33W
Portage la Prairie town 39 49.58N 98.20W
Portalegre 13 39.17N 7.25W
Port Alfred 54 33.36S 26.52E
Port Angeles 40 48.06N123.26W
Port Antonio 43 18.10N 76.27W
Port Arthur 35 43.08S147.50E
Port Augusta 36 32.30S137.46E
Port-au-Prince 43 18.33N 72.20W
Portbou 13 42.25N 3.09E
Port Chalmers 29 45.49S170.37E
Port Elizabeth 54 33.57S 25.34E
Port Ellen 11 55.38N 6.12W
Port Erin 8 54.05N 4.45W
Port Gentil 52 0.40S 8.46E
Portglenone 10 54.53N 6.30W
Port Harcourt 50 4.43N 7.05E

Porthcawl 9 51.28N 3.42W
Port Hedland 32 20.24S118.36E
Porthmadog 8 52.55N 4.08W
Port Huron 44 42.59N 82.28W
Portimão 13 37.08N 8.32W
Portland Maine 44 43.39N 70.17W
Portland Oreg. 40 45.32N122.40W
Puncak Laoise 10 53.03N 7.20W
Port Lincoln 36 34.43S135.49E
Port Macquarie 37 31.28S152.25E
Portmarnock 10 53.25N 6.09W
Port Moresby 34 9.30S147.07E
Portnaguiran 11 58.15N 6.10W
Port-Nouveau Québec 39 58.35N 65.59W
Porto 13 41.09N 8.37W
Pôrto Alegre 45 30.03S 51.10W
Pôrto Alexandre 52 15.55S 11.51E
Porto Esperança 45 19.36S 57.24W
Port of Spain 43 10.38N 61.31W
Pôrtom 18 62.42N 21.37E
Porton 9 51.08N 1.44W
Porto-Novo 50 6.30N 2.47E
Port Torres 14 40.49N 8.24E
Porto Vecchio 12 41.35N 9.16E
Pôrto Velho 46 8.45S 63.54W
Portpatrick 11 54.51N 5.07W
Port Phillip B. 37 38.05S144.50E
Port Pirie 36 33.11S138.01E
Portree 11 57.24N 6.12W
Portrush 10 55.12N 6.40W
Port St. Louis 12 43.25N 4.40E
Portsmouth 9 50.48N 1.06W
Portsoy 11 57.41N 2.41W
Portstewart 10 55.11N 6.43W
Port Sudan see Bur Südān 51
Port Talbot 9 51.35N 3.48W
Portugal 13 39.30N 8.05W
Port Vendres 12 42.31N 3.06E
Posadas 48 27.25S 55.48W
Posse 45 14.05S 46.22W
Postmasburg 54 28.19S 23.03E
Potchefstroom 54 26.42S 27.05E
Potenza 14 40.40N 15.47E
Potgietersrus 54 24.11S 29.00E
Poti 47 5.01S 42.48W
Potiskum 50 11.40N 11.03E
Potosí 48 19.35S 65.45W
Potsdam 16 52.24N 13.04E
Pottstown 44 40.15N 75.38W
Povorino 21 51.12N 42.15E
Powder r. 40 46.40N105.15W
Powell, L. 40 37.30N110.45W
Powys d. 9 52.26N 3.26W
Požarevac 17 44.38N 21.12E
Poznań 16 52.25N 16.53E
Pozoblanco 13 38.23N 4.51W
Prachuap Kiri Khan 27 11.50N 99.49E
Prades 12 42.38N 2.25E
Prague see Praha 16
Praha 16 50.05N 14.25E
Prato 14 43.52N 11.06E
Preesall 8 53.55N 2.58W
Prescott Ariz. 40 34.34N112.28W
Presidencia Roque Sáenz Peña 48 26.50S 60.30W
Presidente Epitácio 45 21.56S 52.07W
Presidente Prudente 45 22.09S 51.24W
Prespa, L. 15 40.53N 21.02E
Presteigne 9 52.17N 3.00W
Preston 8 53.46N 2.42W
Preston Idaho 40 42.06N111.53W
Prestonpans 11 55.57N 3.00W
Prestwick 11 55.30N 4.36W
Pretoria 54 25.43S 28.11E
Préveza 15 38.58N 20.43E
Pribram 16 49.42N 14.00E
Prieska 54 29.40S 22.43E
Prilep 15 41.20N 21.32E
Primorsk R.S.F.S.R. 20 60.18N 28.35E
Prince Albert 54 33.14S 22.02E
Prince Albert Sd. 38 70.25N115.00W
Prince Charles I. 39 67.50N 76.00W
Prince Edward Island d. 39 46.15N 63.10W
Prince of Wales, C. 38 66.00N168.30W
Prince of Wales I. 39 73.00N 99.00W
Prince Patrick I. 38 77.00N120.00W
Prince Rupert 38 54.09N130.20W
Princeton Ind. 44 38.21N 87.33W
Príncipe i. 50 1.37N 7.27E
Prinzapolca 43 13.19N 83.35W
Priština 15 42.39N 21.10E
Prizren 15 42.13N 20.42E
Prokopyevsk 22 53.55N 86.45E
Prome 26 18.50N 95.14E
Providence 44 41.50N 71.25W
Provins 12 48.34N 3.18E
Provo 40 40.15N111.40W
Prudhoe Bay town 38 70.20N148.25W
Prüm 16 50.12N 6.25E
Prut r. 17 45.29N 28.14E
Przemyśl 17 49.48N 22.48E
Przhevalsk 22 42.31N 78.22E
Psel r. 21 49.00N 33.30E
Pskov 20 57.48N 28.00E
Puebla 42 19.03N 98.10W
Pueblo 40 38.17N104.38W
Puente-Genil 13 37.24N 4.46W
Puerto Barrios 43 15.41N 88.32W
Puerto Cabezas 43 14.02N 83.24W
Puerto de Santa Maria 13 36.36N 6.14W
Puerto Juárez 43 21.26N 86.51W
Puertollano 13 38.41N 4.07W
Puerto Montt 49 41.28S 72.31W
Puerto Peñasco 42 31.20N113.35W
Puerto Pinasco 45 22.36S 57.50W
Puerto Plata 43 19.48N 70.41W
Puerto Princessa 27 9.46N118.45E
Puerto Quepos 43 9.28N 84.10W
Puerto Rico 43 18.20N 66.30W
Puerto Sastre 45 22.02S 58.00W
Pukaki, L. 29 44.00S170.10E
Pukekohe 29 37.12S174.56E
Pula 16 44.52N 13.53E
Puncak Jaya mtn. 27 4.00S137.15E
Pune 25 18.34N 73.58E
Punjab d. 25 30.45N 75.30E
Puno 46 15.53S 70.03W
Punta Alta 49 38.50S 62.00W
Punta Arenas town 49 53.10S 70.56W
Punta Gorda town 43 16.10N 88.45W
Puntarenas 43 10.00N 84.50W
Pur r. 22 67.30N 75.30E
Purus r. 46 3.58S 61.25W
Pusan 26 35.05N129.02E
Pushkin 20 59.43N 30.22E

Pustoshka 20 56.20N 29.20E
Putao 26 27.22N 97.27E
Putaruru 29 38.03S175.47E
Putumayo r. 46 3.05S 68.10W
Puy de Dôme mtn. 12 45.46N 2.56E
Puysegur Pt. 29 46.10S166.35E
Pweto 53 8.27S 28.52E
Pwllheli 8 52.53N 4.25W
Pyasina r. 23 73.10N 84.55E
Pyatigorsk 21 44.04N 43.06E
Pyhä r. 18 64.28N 24.14E
Pyhäjoki 18 64.28N 24.13E
Pyhäjärvi 18 61.00N 22.20E
Pyinmana 26 19.45N 96.12E
Pyŏngyang 26 39.00N125.47E
Pyramid L. 40 40.00N119.35W
Pyrénées mts. 12 42.40N 0.30E

Q
Qamdo 26 31.11N 97.18E
Qarqan He r. 25 40.56N 86.27E
Qatar 24 25.20N 51.10E
Qattara Depression see Qaṭṭārah, Munkhafaḍ al f. 51
Qaṭṭārah, Munkhafaḍ al f. 51 29.40N 27.30E
Qâyen 24 33.44N 59.07E
Qiemo 25 38.08N 85.33E
Qilian Shan mts. 26 38.30N 99.20E
Qingdao 26 36.02N120.25E
Qingjiang 26 33.35N119.02E
Qiqihar 26 47.23N124.00E
Qishn 24 15.25N 51.40E
Quanzhou 26 24.57N118.36E
Queanbeyan 37 35.24S149.17E
Québec 44 46.50N 71.15W
Québec d. 39 51.00N 70.00W
Quedlinburg 16 51.48N 11.09E
Queen Charlotte Is. 38 53.00N132.30W
Queen Charlotte Str. 38 51.00N129.00W
Queen Elizabeth Is. 39 78.30N 99.00W
Queen Maud G. 39 68.30N 99.00W
Queensland d. 34 23.30S144.00E
Quelimane 53 17.53S 36.57E
Querétaro 42 20.38N100.23W
Quesnel 38 53.03N122.31W
Quetta 25 30.12N 67.00E
Quezaltenango 42 14.50N 91.30W
Quezon City 27 14.39N121.01E
Quibala 52 10.48N 14.56E
Quibaxi 52 8.34S 14.37E
Quiberon 12 47.29N 3.07W
Quilengues 52 14.09S 14.04E
Quilon 25 8.53N 76.38E
Quimbele 52 6.29S 16.25E
Quimper 12 48.00N 4.06W
Quimperlé 12 47.52N 3.33W
Quincy Ill. 41 39.55N 91.22W
Qui Nhon 27 13.47N109.11E
Quinto 13 41.25N 0.30W
Quissanga 53 12.24S 40.33E
Quissico 54 24.42S 34.44E
Quito 46 0.14S 78.30W
Quorn 36 32.20S138.02E

R
Raasay i. 11 57.25N 6.05W
Raba 27 8.27S118.45E
Rabat 50 34.02N 6.51W
Rach Gia 27 10.02N105.05E
Racine 41 42.42N 87.50W
Radebeul 16 51.06N 13.41E
Radom 17 51.26N 21.10E
Radomir 15 42.33N 23.00E
Radstock 9 51.17N 2.25W
Rafaela 48 31.16S 61.44W
Rafsanjan 24 30.24N 56.00E
Ragusa 14 36.56N 14.44E
Rainier, Mt. 40 46.52N121.45W
Raipur 25 21.14N 81.38E
Rājasthān d. 25 26.15N 74.00E
Rajkot 25 22.18N 70.47E
Rakaia r. 29 43.52S172.13E
Rakvere 20 59.22N 26.28E
Raleigh 41 35.46N 78.39W
Rama 43 12.09N 84.15W
Ramelton 10 55.02N 7.40W
Ramos Arizpe 42 25.35N100.59W
Ramsey England 9 52.27N 0.06W
Ramsey I.o.M. 8 54.19N 4.23W
Ramsgate 9 51.20N 1.25E
Rancagua 49 34.10S 70.45W
Rânchi 25 23.21N 85.20E
Randalstown 10 54.45N 6.20W
Randers 19 56.28N 10.03E
Rangiora 29 43.18S172.38E
Rangitaiki r. 29 37.55S176.50E
Rangoon 27 16.47N 96.10E
Rannes, Loch 11 56.41N 4.20W
Rann of Kutch f. 25 23.50N 69.50E
Rapallo 14 44.20N 9.14E
Rapid City 40 44.06N103.14W
Rarotonga i. 30 21.14S159.46W
Rasht 24 37.18N 49.38E
Rathcormack 10 52.05N 8.18W
Rathdrum 10 52.56N 6.15W
Rathenow 16 52.37N 12.21E
Rathlin I. 10 55.17N 6.15W
Rath Luirc 10 52.21N 8.41W
Rathmullen 10 55.06N 7.32W
Raton 40 36.54N104.27W
Rattray Head 11 57.37N 1.50W
Rättvik 19 60.53N 15.06E
Rauma r. 18 62.32N 7.43E
Ravena 40 42.26N 86.51W
Ravenna 14 44.25N 12.12E
Ravensburg 16 47.47N 9.37E
Rawalpindi 25 33.36N 73.04E
Rawlinna 33 30.01S125.21E
Rawlins 40 41.46N107.16W
Razgrad 17 43.32N 26.30E
Ré, Île de i. 12 46.10N 1.26W
Reading 9 51.27N 0.57W
Recife 47 8.06S 34.53W
Reconquista 48 29.08S 59.38W
Red r. Canada 39 50.30N 96.50W
Red r. U.S.A. 41 31.10N 92.00W
Red Basin f. see Sichuan Pendi f. 26
Redbridge 9 51.35N 0.08E
Redcar 8 54.37N 1.04W
Redding 40 40.35N122.24W
Redditch 9 52.18N 1.57W
Red Lake town 39 50.59N 93.40W
Redruth 9 50.14N 5.14W
Red Sea 24 20.00N 39.00E
Ree, Lough 10 53.31N 7.58W
Regensburg 16 49.01N 12.07E
Reggane 50 26.30N 0.30E
Reggio Calabria 14 38.07N 15.38E

Reggio Emilia-Romagna 14 44.40N 10.37E
Regina 38 50.30N104.38W
Reigate 9 51.14N 0.13W
Reims 12 49.15N 4.02E
Reindeer L. 38 57.00N102.20W
Rendsburg 16 54.19N 9.39E
Rengat 27 0.26S102.35E
Reni 17 45.28N 28.17E
Renmark 36 34.10S140.45E
Rennes 12 48.06N 1.40W
Reno r. 14 44.36N 12.17E
Reno 40 39.32N119.49W
Republican r. 41 39.05N 94.50W
Republic of Ireland 10 53.00N 8.00W
Republic of South Africa 54 28.30S 24.50E
Requena 46 5.05S 73.52W
Resistencia 48 27.28S 59.00W
Resolute 39 74.40N 95.00W
Rethel 15 49.31N 4.22E
Réthimnon 15 35.22N 24.29E
Reus 15 41.10N 1.06E
Reutlingen 16 48.29N 9.13E
Revelstoke 38 51.02N118.12W
Revue r. 54 19.58S 34.40E
Reykjavík 18 64.09N 21.58W
Rēzekne 20 56.30N 27.22E
Rhayader 9 52.19N 3.30W
Rhein r. 16 51.53N 6.03E
Rheine 16 52.17N 7.26E
Rhine see Rhein r. 16
Rhinelander 41 45.39N 89.23W
Rhino Camp 53 3.00N 31.20E
Rhode Island d. 44 41.40N 71.30W
Rhodes i. see Ródhos i. 15
Rhondda 9 51.39N 3.30W
Rhône r. 12 43.25N 4.45E
Rhosllanerchrugog 8 53.01N 3.04W
Rhum i. 11 57.00N 6.20W
Rhyl 8 53.19N 3.29W
Ribadeo 13 43.32N 7.04W
Ribauè 53 14.55S 38.27E
Ribble r. 8 53.45N 2.44W
Ribeirão Prêto 45 21.09S 47.48W
Ribérac 12 45.14N 0.22E
Richland 40 46.20N119.17W
Richmond U.K. 8 54.24N 1.43W
Richmond Va. 41 37.34N 77.27W
Riesa 16 51.18N 13.18E
Rieti 14 42.24N 12.53E
Riga 19 56.53N 24.08E
Riga, G. of see Rīgas Jūras Līcis g. 19
Rīgas Jūras Līcis g. 19 57.30N 23.35E
Riihimäki 19 60.45N 24.46E
Rimah, Wādi ar r. 24 26.10N 44.00E
Rimini 14 44.01N 12.34E
Ringkøbing 19 56.05N 8.15E
Ringwood 37 37.51S145.13E
Riobamba 46 1.44S 78.40W
Rio Branco 46 9.59S 67.49W
Río Claro 45 22.19S 47.35W
Rio de Janeiro 45 22.53S 43.17W
Rio Gallegos 49 51.35S 69.15W
Río Grande r. 45 32.03S 52.08W
Río Grande r. 42 25.55N 97.08W
Rio Grande town 45 32.03S 52.08W
Río Verde town 42 21.56N100.55W
Ripley N.Y. 44 42.16N 79.43W
Ripon 8 54.08N 1.31W
Riraporã 45 17.20S 45.02W
Risør 19 61.03N 4.54E
Riverina f. 37 34.30S145.20E
Riversdale 54 34.05S 21.15E
Riyadh see Ar Riyāḍ 24
Rize 21 41.03N 40.31E
Rjukan 19 59.52N 8.34E
Roag, Loch 11 58.14N 6.50W
Roanne 12 46.02N 4.05E
Roanoke r. 41 36.00N 76.35W
Robin Hood's Bay town 8 54.26N 0.31W
Robinvale 36 34.37S142.50E
Roboré 48 18.20S 59.45W
Robson, Mt. 38 53.00N119.09W
Rocha 49 34.30S 54.22W
Rochdale 8 53.36N 2.10W
Rochechouart 12 45.49N 0.50E
Rochefort 12 45.57N 0.58W
Rochester Minn. 41 44.01N 92.27W
Rochester N.Y. 44 43.12N 77.37W
Rockford 41 42.16N 89.06W
Rockhampton 34 23.22S150.32E
Rockland Mich. 44 46.44N 89.12W
Rocklands Resr. 36 37.13S141.52E
Rock Springs Wyo. 40 41.35N109.13W
Rockville 44 39.05N 77.09W
Rodel 11 57.44N 6.58W
Ródhos i. 15 36.12N 28.00E
Ródhos 15 36.26N 28.13E
Rolla Mo. 41 37.56N 91.55W
Roma 14 41.54N 12.29E
Romaine r. 39 50.20N 63.45W
Romania 17 46.30N 24.00E
Romano, C. 41 25.50N 81.42W
Romans 12 45.03N 5.03E
Rome see Roma 14
Romilly 12 48.31N 3.44E
Romney Marsh f. 9 51.03N 0.55E
Rona i. 11 57.33N 5.58W
Ronda 13 36.45N 5.10W
Rondônopolis 47 16.29S 54.37W
Rönne 19 55.06N 14.42E
Roodepoort 54 26.08N 27.51E
Roof Butte mtn. 40 36.28N109.05W
Roosendaal 16 51.32N 4.28E
Roosevelt r. 46 7.35S 60.20W
Ropcha 20 62.50N 51.55E
Roper r. 34 14.40S134.30W
Roper Valley town 34 14.56S134.00E
Roraima, Mt. 46 5.14N 60.44W
Röros 18 62.35N 11.23E
Rosa, Monte mtn. 16 45.56N 7.51E
Rosario 48 32.57S 60.40W
Roscoff 12 48.44N 4.00W
Roscommon d. 10 53.38N 8.13W
Roscrea 10 52.57N 7.49W
Roseau 43 15.18N 61.23W
Roseburg 40 43.13N123.21W
Rosenheim 16 47.51N 12.09E
Roskilde 19 55.39N 12.07E
Roslags-Näsby 19 59.26N 18.04E
Roslavl 20 53.55N 32.53E
Rosslare 10 52.17N 6.23W
Ross-on-Wye 9 51.55N 2.36W
Rostock 16 54.06N 12.09E
Rostov R.S.F.S.R. 21 47.15N 39.45E
Rothbury 8 55.19N 1.54W
Rotherham 8 53.26N 1.21W
Rothes 11 57.31N 3.13W
Rothesay 11 55.50N 5.03W

Roti i. 27 10.30S123.10E
Roto 37 33.04S145.27E
Rotorua 29 38.09S176.17E
Rotorua, L. 29 38.00S176.00E
Rotterdam 16 51.55N 4.29E
Roubaix 12 50.42N 3.10E
Rouen 12 49.26N 1.05E
Round Mt. 37 30.26S152.15E
Roundup 40 46.27N108.34W
Rouyn 44 48.14N 79.01W
Rovaniemi 18 66.30N 25.40E
Rovinj 16 45.06N 13.39E
Rovno 17 50.39N 26.10E
Roxburgh 29 45.33S169.19E
Royale, Isle i. 44 48.00N 89.00W
Royal Leamington Spa 9 52.18N 1.32W
Royal Tunbridge Wells 9 51.07N 0.16E
Royston 9 52.03N 0.01W
Rtishchevo 20 52.16N 43.45E
Ruahine Range mts. 29 40.00S176.00E
Ruapehu 29 39.20S175.30E
Ruapuke I. 29 46.45S168.30E
Rubi r. 52 2.50N 24.06E
Rudolstadt 16 50.44N 11.20E
Ruffec 12 46.02N 0.12E
Rufino 49 34.16S 62.45W
Rugby 9 52.23N 1.16W
Ruhr r. 16 51.27N 6.41E
Rukwa, L. 53 8.00S 32.20E
Ruma 17 44.59N 19.51E
Rum Cay i. 43 23.41N 74.53W
Runcorn 8 53.20N 2.44W
Rungwa r. 53 7.38S 31.00E
Rungwe Mt. 53 9.10S 33.40E
Ruo Shui r. 26 42.15N101.03E
Rusape 54 18.30S 32.08E
Ruse 15 43.50N 25.59E
Rushden 9 52.17N 0.37W
Rustavi 21 41.34N 45.03E
Rustenburg 54 25.39S 27.13E
Rutana 53 3.58S 30.00E
Ruteng 27 8.35S120.28E
Ruthin 8 53.07N 3.18W
Rutland 44 43.36N 72.59W
Rutshuru 53 1.10S 29.26E
Ruvu r. 53 6.50S 38.42E
Ruvuma r. 53 10.30S 40.30E
Ruwenzori Range mts. 53 0.30N 30.00E
Ruyigi 53 3.26S 30.14E
Ruzayevka 20 54.04N 44.55E
Rwanda 53 2.00S 30.00E
Ryan, Loch 11 54.56N 5.02W
Ryazan 20 54.37N 39.43E
Ryazhsk 20 53.40N 40.07E
Rye 9 50.57N 0.46E
Rye r. 8 54.10N 0.44W
Rzeszów 17 50.04N 22.00E
Rzhev 20 56.15N 34.18E

S
Saale r. 16 51.58N 11.53E
Saarbrücken 16 49.15N 6.58E
Saarijärvi 18 62.43N 25.16E
Saba i. 43 17.42N 63.26W
Šabac 17 44.45N 19.41E
Sabadell 13 41.33N 2.07E
Sabi r. 54 21.16S 32.20E
Sabinas 42 28.30N101.10W
Sabinas Hidalgo 42 26.33N100.10W
Sabine r. 41 29.40N 93.50W
Sable I. 39 44.00N 60.00W
Sacedón 13 40.29N 2.44W
Sacramento 40 38.32N121.30W
Sacramento r. 40 38.05N122.00W
Sádaba 13 42.19N 1.10W
Sadani 53 6.00S 38.40E
Sadiya 25 27.49N 95.38E
Säffle 19 59.08N 12.56E
Saffron Walden 9 52.02N 0.15E
Safi 50 32.20N 9.17W
Sagaing 25 21.52N 95.59E
Sagamihara 28 35.32N139.23E
Saginaw 44 43.25N 83.54W
Saglouc 39 62.10N 75.40W
Sagua la Grande 43 22.55N 80.05W
Saguenay r. 39 48.10N 69.45W
Sagunto 13 39.40N 0.17W
Sahagún 13 42.23N 5.02W
Sahara des. 50 23.00N 12.00E
Sa'īdābād 24 29.28N 55.43E
Saidpur 25 25.48N 88.54E
Saimbeyli 21 38.07N 36.08E
St. Abb's Head 11 55.54N 2.07W
St. Albans 9 51.46N 0.21W
St. Amand-Mont-Rond town 12 46.43N 2.29E
St. Andrews 11 56.20N 2.48W
St. Ann's Bay town 43 18.26N 77.12W
St. Anthony 39 51.24N 55.37W
St. Arnaud 36 36.40S143.20E
St. Augustine 41 29.54N 81.19W
St. Austell 9 50.20N 4.48W
St. Bees Head 8 54.31N 3.39W
St. Brides B. 9 51.48N 5.03W
St. Brieuc 12 48.31N 2.45W
St. Catharines 44 43.10N 79.15W
St. Catherine's Pt. 9 50.34N 1.18W
St. Céré 12 44.52N 1.53E
St. Cloud 41 45.34N 94.10W
St. David's 9 51.54N 5.16W
St. David's Head 9 51.55N 5.19W
St. Denis 12 48.56N 2.21E
St. Dié 12 48.17N 6.57E
St. Dizier 12 48.38N 4.58E
St. Elias, Mt. 38 60.20N139.00W
Saintes 12 45.44N 0.38W
St. Étienne 12 45.26N 4.26E
Saintfield 10 54.28N 5.50W
St. Flour 12 45.02N 3.05E
St. Gallen 16 47.25N 9.23E
St. George's 43 12.04N 61.44W
St. George's Channel 10 51.30N 6.20W
St. Germain 12 48.53N 2.04E
St. Girons 12 42.59N 1.08E
St. Gotthard Pass 16 46.30N 8.55E
St. Govan's Head 9 51.36N 4.55W
St. Helena B. 54 32.35S 18.05E
St. Helens 8 53.28N 2.43W
St. Helier 9 49.12N 2.07W
St. Hyacinthe 44 45.38N 72.57W
St. Ives 9 50.13N 5.29W
St. Jean Pied-de-Port 12 43.10N 1.14W
St. John 44 45.16N 66.03W
St. John r. 44 45.15N 66.04W

St. John's Antigua 43 17.07N 61.51W
St. John's Canada 39 47.34N 52.41W
St. John's Pt. 10 54.14N 5.39W
St. Joseph Mo. 41 39.45N 94.51W
St. Lawrence r. 44 48.45N 68.30W
St. Lawrence, G. of 39 48.00N 62.00W
St. Lawrence I. 38 63.00N170.00W
St. Lô 12 49.07N 1.05W
St. Louis 41 38.40N 90.15W
St. Lucia 43 14.05N 61.00W
St. Malo 12 48.39N 2.00W
St.-Marc 43 19.08N 72.41W
St. Margaret's Hope 11 58.49N 2.57W
St. Martin i. 43 18.05N 63.05W
St. Martin's i. 9 49.57N 6.16W
St. Mary 9 49.14N 2.10W
St. Marys 35 41.33S148.12E
St. Mary's i. 9 49.55N 6.16W
St. Maurice r. 44 46.21N 72.31W
St. Moritz 16 46.30N 9.51E
St. Nazaire 12 47.17N 2.12W
St. Neots 9 52.14N 0.16W
St. Omer 12 50.45N 2.15E
St. Paul Minn. 41 45.00N 93.10W
St. Peter Port 9 49.27N 2.32W
St. Petersburg 41 27.45N 82.40W
St. Pierre and Miquelon i. 39 47.00N 56.15W
St. Pölten 16 48.13N 15.37E
St. Quentin 12 49.51N 3.17E
St. Thomas 44 42.47N 81.12W
St. Tropez 12 43.16N 6.39E
St. Vallier 12 45.11N 4.49E
St. Vincent, G. 36 35.00S138.05E
St. Vincent and the Grenadines 43 13.00N 61.15W
St. Vith 16 50.15N 6.08E
St. Yrieix 12 45.31N 1.12E
Sakai 28 34.35N135.28E
Sakania 53 12.45S 28.34E
Sakarya r. 21 41.08N 30.36E
Sakhalin i. 23 51.00N143.00E
Sakrivier 54 30.53S 20.24E
Sal r. 21 47.33N 40.40E
Sala 19 59.55N 16.36E
Salado r. Buenos Aires 49 35.44S 57.22W
Salado r. Santa Fé 49 31.40S 60.41W
Salado r. La Pampa 49 36.15S 66.55W
Salālah 24 17.00N 54.04E
Salamanca 13 40.58N 5.40W
Salbris 17 47.26N 2.03E
Salcombe 9 50.14N 3.47W
Sale 37 38.06S147.06E
Salem 25 11.38N 78.08E
Salerno 14 40.41N 14.45E
Salerno, Golfo di g. 14 40.30N 14.45E
Salford 8 53.30N 2.17W
Salima 53 13.45S 34.26E
Salina Cruz 42 16.11N 95.12W
Salins 12 46.56N 5.53E
Salisbury 9 51.04N 1.48W
Salisbury Plain f. 9 51.15N 1.55W
Salmon 40 45.11N113.54W
Salmon River Mts. 40 44.30N114.30W
Salo 19 60.23N 23.08E
Salobreña 13 36.45N 3.35W
Salon 12 43.38N 5.06E
Salonga r. 52 0.09S 19.52E
Salsk 21 46.30N 41.33E
Salso r. 14 37.07N 13.57E
Salt r. 40 33.23N112.18W
Salta 48 24.47S 65.24W
Saltee Is. 10 52.08N 6.36W
Saltfleet 8 53.25N 0.11E
Salt Lake City 40 40.45N111.55W
Saltillo 42 25.30N101.00W
Salto 49 31.23S 57.58W
Salto da Divisa 47 16.04S 40.00W
Salvador 47 12.58S 38.29W
Salween r. 27 16.32N 97.35E
Salyany 21 39.36N 48.59E
Salzburg 16 47.54N 13.03E
Samaná 43 19.14N 69.20W
Samar i. 27 11.45N125.15E
Samarinda 27 0.30S117.09E
Samarkand 22 39.40N 66.57E
Sambalpur 25 21.27N 83.58E
Sambre r. 12 50.29N 4.52E
Same 53 4.10S 37.43E
Samoa is. 30 14.20S170.00W
Samoa Is. 30 14.00S171.00W
Sámos i. 15 37.44N 26.45E
Samothráki i. 15 40.26N 25.35E
Sampit 27 2.34S112.59E
Şamşun 21 41.17N 36.22E
Şan'ā' 24 15.23N 44.14E
Sana r. 16 45.03N 16.23E
Sanaga r. 50 3.35N 9.40E
San Antonio 40 29.25N 98.30W
San Antonio Oeste 49 40.44S 64.57W
San Bernardino 40 34.07N117.18W
San Blas, C. 41 29.40N 85.20W
San Carlos de Bariloche 49 41.08S 71.15W
San Cristóbal 46 7.46N 72.15W
Sancti Spíritus 43 21.55N 79.28W
Sanda i. 11 55.17N 5.34W
Sandakan 27 5.52N118.04E
Sanday i. 11 59.15N 2.33W
Sandgate 37 27.18S153.00E
San Diego 40 32.45N117.10W
Sandnes 19 58.51N 5.44E
Sandness 11 60.18N 1.38W
Sandoa 52 9.41S 22.56E
Sandoway 26 18.28N 94.20E
Sandown 9 50.39N 1.09W
Sandpoint town 40 48.17N116.34W
Sandringham 8 52.50N 0.30E
Sandusky Ohio 44 41.27N 82.42W
Sandviken 19 60.37N 16.46E
San Fernando de Apure 46 7.35N 67.15W
San Francisco 40 37.45N122.27W
San Francisco, C. 46 0.50N 80.05W
San Francisco de Macorís 43 19.19N 70.15W
Sangha r. 52 1.10S 16.47E
Sangonera r. 13 37.58N 1.04W
San Gottardo, Passo del pass 16 46.30N 8.55E
San José 43 9.59N 84.04W
San José de Chiquitos 48 17.53S 60.45W
San José de Mayo 49 34.20S 56.42W

San Juan 43 18.29N 66.08W
San Juan r. 40 37.20N110.05W
San Juan del Norte 43 10.58N 83.40W
San Juan Mts. 40 37.30N107.00W
Sankuru r. 52 4.20S 20.27E
San Leonardo 13 41.49N 3.04W
Sanlúcar de Barrameda 13 36.46N 6.21W
San Luis Obispo 40 35.16N120.40W
San Luis Potosí 42 22.10N101.00W
San Marino 14 43.55N 12.27E
San Matías, Golfo g. 49 41.30S 64.00W
San Miguel 43 13.28N 88.10W
San Miguel de Tucumán 48 26.49S 65.13W
San Nicolas 49 33.20S 60.13W
San Pedro Sula 43 15.26N 88.01W
San Pietro i. 14 39.09N 8.16E
Sanquhar 11 55.22N 3.56W
San Remo 14 43.48N 7.46E
San Salvador 43 24.00N 74.32W
San Salvador 43 13.40N 89.10W
San Sebastián 13 43.19N 1.59W
San Severo 14 41.40N 15.24E
Santa Ana 40 33.44N117.54W
Santa Barbara 42 26.48N105.49W
Santa Barbara 40 34.25N119.41W
Santa Clara 43 22.25N 79.58W
Santa Cruz r. 49 50.03S 68.35W
Santa Cruz Bolivia 48 17.45S 63.14W
Santa Cruz Canary Is. 50 28.27N 16.14W
Santa Cruz Is. 30 10.30S166.00E
Santa Elena, C. 43 10.54N 85.56W
Santa Fé 43 31.40S 60.40W
Santa Fe 40 35.41N105.57W
Santa Maria 40 34.56N120.25W
Santana do Livramento 49 30.53S 55.31W
Santander 13 43.28N 3.48W
Santañy 13 39.20N 3.07E
Santarém 47 2.26S 54.41W
Santa Rosa Calif. 40 38.26N122.43W
Santa Rosalía 42 27.20N112.20W
Santiago 49 33.27S 70.40W
Santiago r. 46 4.30S 77.48W
Santiago de Compostela 13 42.52N 8.33W
Santiago de Cuba 43 20.00N 75.49W
Santiago del Estero 48 27.50S 64.15W
Santo André 45 23.39S 46.29W
Santo Angelo 45 28.18S 54.16W
Santo Domingo 43 18.30N 69.57W
Santos 45 23.56S 46.22W
Santo Tomé 48 28.31S 56.03W
San Vicente 43 13.38N 88.42W
Sanza Pombo 52 7.20S 16.12E
São Borja 45 28.35S 56.01W
São Carlos 45 22.01S 47.54W
São Francisco r. 47 10.30S 36.20W
São Francisco do Sul 45 26.17S 48.39W
São João del Rei 45 21.08S 44.15W
São José do Rio Prêto 45 20.50S 49.20W
São José dos Campos 45 23.07S 45.52W
São Leopoldo 45 29.46S 51.09W
São Luís 47 2.34S 44.16W
São Miguel d'Oeste 45 26.45S 53.34W
Saône r. 12 45.46N 4.52E
São Paulo 45 23.33S 46.39W
São Paulo d. 45 22.05S 48.00W
São Paulo de Olivença 46 3.34S 68.55W
São Tomé i. 50 0.19N 6.43E
São Tomé & Príncipe 50 1.00N 7.00E
São Vicente 45 23.57S 46.23W
Sapporo 26 43.05N141.21E
Sapri 14 40.04N 15.38E
Sara Buri 27 14.30N100.50E
Sarajevo 17 43.52N 18.26E
Saransk 20 54.12N 45.10E
Saratov 21 51.30N 45.55E
Sarbäz 24 26.39N 61.20E
Sardegna i. 14 40.00N 9.00E
Sardinia i. see Sardegna i. 14
Sargodha 25 32.01N 72.40E
Sarh 50 9.08N 18.22E
Sark i. 9 49.26N 2.22W
Sarmi 21 1.51S138.45E
Sarmiento 49 45.35S 69.05W
Särna 19 61.41N 13.08E
Sarnia 44 42.58N 82.23W
Sarpsborg 19 59.17N 11.07E
Sarrebourg 12 48.43N 7.03E
Sarria 13 42.47N 7.25W
Sarthe r. 12 47.29N 0.30W
Saskatchewan d. 38 55.00N105.00W
Saskatchewan r. 39 53.25N100.15W
Saskatoon 38 52.10N106.40W
Sasovo 20 54.21N 41.58E
Sassandra 50 4.58N 6.08W
Sassari 14 40.43N 8.33E
Sassnitz 16 54.32N 13.40E
Satu Mare 17 47.48N 22.52E
Sauda 19 59.39N 6.20E
Saudi Arabia 24 26.00N 44.00E
Saulieu 12 47.17N 4.14E
Sault Sainte Marie Canada 44 46.31N 84.20W
Sault Sainte Marie U.S.A. 44 46.29N 84.22W
Saumlaki 34 7.59S131.22E
Saumur 12 47.16N 0.05W
Saurimo 52 9.38S 20.20E
Sava r. 17 44.50N 20.26E
Savannah r. 41 32.09N 81.01W
Savannah Ga. 41 32.09N 81.01W
Savé 50 8.04N 2.37E
Save r. 54 20.59S 35.02E
Savona 14 44.18N 8.28E
Savonlinna 20 61.52N 28.51E
Sawston 9 52.07N 0.11E
Saxmundham 9 52.13N 1.29E
Saynshand 26 44.58N110.12E
Sayula 42 19.52N103.36W
Sázova r. 16 49.53N 14.21E
Scafell Pike mtn. 8 54.27N 3.12W
Scalloway 11 60.08N 1.17W
Scammon Bay town 38 61.50N165.35W
Scapa Flow str. 11 58.53N 3.05W
Scarborough 8 54.17N 0.24W
Schaffhausen 16 47.42N 8.38E
Schelde r. 16 51.13N 4.25E
Schenectady 44 42.47N 73.53W
Schleswig 16 54.32N 9.34E